Reminisce
Around the Table
FOND MEMORIES OF FOOD, FAMILY AND FRIENDS

table of contents

page 6

page 32

page 54

page 72

page 88

page 104

page 122

page 142

page 164

REMINISCE AROUND THE TABLE

Catherine Cassidy **Vice President, Editor-in-Chief**
Heidi Reuter Lloyd **Vice President, Executive Editor/Books**
Mark Hagen **Sr. Editor/Books**
Julie Schnittka **Project Editor**
Krista Lanphier, Michelle Rozumalski **Contributing Editors**
Sharon K. Nelson **Creative Director, Home & Garden**
Edwin Robles, Jr. **Associate Creative Director**
Angie Packer **Project Art Director**
Raeann Sundholm **Contributing Art Director**
Julie Wagner **Content Production Manager**
Kathy Crawford **Layout Designer**
Deb Warlaumont Mulvey **Copy Chief**
Susan Uphill **Copy Editor**
Trudi Bellin **Photo Coordinator**
Mary Ann Koebernik **Assistant Photo Coordinator**
Barb Czysz **Administrative Assistant**

Heather Lamb **Executive Editor, *Reminisce***
Bettina Miller **Editor, *Reminisce***
Cheryl A. Michalek **Art Director, *Reminisce***
John Burlingham **Senior Editor, *Reminisce***
Blanche Comiskey, Melody Trick **Editorial Assistants, *Reminisce***

Lisa Karpinski **North American Chief Marketing Officer**
Dan Fink **Vice President/Book Marketing**
Jim Palmen **Creative Director/Creative Marketing**

———————————————

THE READER'S DIGEST ASSOCIATION, INC.
Tom Williams President and Chief Executive Officer
Suzanne M. Grimes Executive Vice President, RDA, and President, Lifestyle Communities

———————————————

REMINISCE BOOKS
©2011 Reiman Media Group, LLC
5400 S. 60th St., Greendale WI 53129-1404

International Standard Book Number (10): 0-89821-905-1
International Standard Book Number (13): 978-0-89821-905-0

Library of Congress Control Number: 2011929211
All rights reserved. Printed in U.S.A.

Cover photo: Classicstock.com
Back cover photos (left to right): Classicstock.com, Superstock

For additional copies of this book or information on other books, write:
Reminisce Customer Service
P.O. Box 5294
Harlan IA 53593-0794
Call toll-free: 1-800/344-6913

Visit our Web site at *reminisce.com*

"Around the Table..."

These familiar words seem so simple. Still, have you ever noticed how memories of sitting around the table, sharing a meal, are often extra special? Of course, a lot of those memories stay with us because of the exceptional food involved...and the fact that such meals were most likely lovingly prepared by Mom or Grandma.

If you were crazy for Mom's homemade Chocolate Dream Layer Torte, and you tried to make the same recipe years later, it probably wasn't the same. There's just no way to completely re-create this slice of life. But throughout the pages of *Reminisce Around the Table*, we help bring back those cherished times.

As kids, we also learned a lot at dinnertime, such as thankfulness ("God bless this food"), manners ("Don't chew with your mouth open") and etiquette ("May I please be excused?"). We even learned the art of engaging conversation ("So, tell us about your day").

Whether it was a Wednesday night supper when you tried to slip your peas to the dog or a holiday meal with candles and good china, the act of eating together became dear to us because of its tradition.

Decades later, when we're older, we tend to look back and appreciate gatherings so much more. You take it for granted as a kid, but later, when families have spread out and some of those we loved have passed away, thoughts of forks clinking on plates and happy chatter around the table become heartfelt memories.

Stories about home cooking, picnics and parties, preparing a treasured family recipe or venturing out to dine are favorites of *Reminisce* readers. We just love to rehash stories from the kitchen, and this book serves up something for everyone.

It's filled with our readers' best stories and photos celebrating joyful times around the table as well as the menus and foods they cherished most. We've also included a journal section where you can jot down your own fond memories, creating a unique keepsake for future generations.

We hope you enjoy this warm, delightful and delicious trip down memory lane.

Best to you all,

Bettina

Bettina Miller
Editor, *Reminisce* magazine

PARTY GIRL. Bettina celebrates birthdays as a youngster.

CHAPTER ONE

Tales from the Table

From celebrating holidays and laughing with neighbors to learning life lessons and discussing serious issues, the kitchen table is the center of the family circle during times of joy...and trouble.

"I can still picture the old round oak table that my family had when I was a child," says Margaret Crill of Nampa, Idaho.

"When Mother announced, 'Come and eat!' three times a day, all 10 members of the family happily headed to our appointed places.

"After the dinner dishes were cleared in the evening, my parents, siblings and I would gather again at the table to read or do homework by the dim light of the kerosene lamp.

"During the air raid drills of World War II, we'd come together at the table in the dark kitchen until the drill was over and the lamp could again be lit. Although we kids were scared, we found peace and comfort around our trusty table."

Turn the page for a selection of more table-side stories that are fixtures in our memories...

mealtimes were magical

By Marthe Hildreth
Sarasota, Florida

Meals were happy times at our Liverpool, New York, home in the '50s. At suppertime, when we were all at the table, Mom and Dad helped us sort out whatever problems we had.

Sometimes there were tears of sorrow over things we had done...or tears of guilt...or even tears of relief when one of our worries had been easily made right or we'd been forgiven for something.

But my greatest memories are the fun times when tears of joy streamed down my face.

One night during the early days of TV, my sister, Melissa, and I came to the table singing part of a silly song we'd just heard that said "no one can make me laugh."

We challenged our parents to do this, and as they told jokes and stories and made faces, Melissa broke down in gales of giggles.

I was determined to remain stoic, and nothing could make me laugh. I even surprised myself when I didn't crack, even though I was bubbling over inside.

Buttered Up a Laugh

We were almost done eating, and I had nearly won when Dad reached over to the butter dish with his knife and scooped up a big dollop. It was summer and the butter was practically melted.

"So no one can make you laugh, eh?" he said, with the knife poised in his hand. "Let's see."

He pulled the knife blade back and let the butter fly across the table, right into my wide-eyed, disbelieving face.

The butter covered my face and part of my hair. Some even flew onto the wall and into the parakeet cage behind me.

I was helpless. I laughed until I cried. The family joined in, and my tears oozed from under the butter and fell on my plate.

BIRD FOOD. Marthe Hildreth (shown with her pet parakeet) had plenty of family fun at the kitchen table.

Sounds of laughter filled the kitchen and each time someone glanced at me, the giggles resumed.

Another night, Melissa and I begged Dad to give us his "peanut butter smile." That's what he called it when he took out his dentures and grinned at us.

Sometimes when I least expected it, the shallow drawer under the table ledge would slowly, mysteriously open by itself right in front of me.

He wouldn't do it, though, saying he wasn't in the mood. We pleaded, but he kept saying no.

Finally he said he would if Melissa, Mom and I all closed our eyes real tight and no one peeked.

We agreed and shut our eyes. He made us wait for what seemed like a long time, then told us he was ready.

Sure enough, he gave us his special smile, then we all laughed appreciatively and went back to our dessert.

Mom picked up her coffee cup and raised it to her lips, and it was a good thing she looked before she drank. There inside the cup, barely covered with coffee, was Daddy's grinning bottom plate!

Then the laughter really began.

In the years before Melissa was old enough to join us, the table was a magical place for me. Mom, Dad and I lingered there, and sometimes when I least expected it, the shallow drawer under the table ledge would slowly, mysteriously open by itself right in front of me. On my birthday, it held a small gift. At Christmas, it had a candy cane.

I didn't figure out how the drawer slid open until I saw a similar table in a used furniture store.

Then it struck me: Dad surreptitiously put his foot up and pushed the drawer open from the opposite side of the table.

Hiding in Plain Sight

I really felt silly when I discovered his trick, but no sillier than I always did when we played the chocolate baby game.

Sometimes after supper, Dad hid one of those tiny chocolate candies in the shape of a baby doll. He'd put it in plain sight, and the first one to see it could have it.

He'd place it on the opposite side of the sugar bowl or under a plate rim, so we never had to leave the table to find it. He probably thought this would eventually develop our observation skills.

I never saw the chocolate baby first, even when he hid it on top of the milk bottle cap right in front of me.

So it must have been out of pity one night, after everyone else had found the chocolate baby at least three times, when out popped the magic drawer and there, in plain sight, was a chocolate baby...just for me.

table manners mattered

At Grandmother Ferguson's ranch house in South Texas in the '30s, the men were always fed first so they could return to work in the fields.

The women of the family waited the table and made sure the men were treated royally. Then, when my father and uncles had their fill, the women sat down and ate.

All this time, my cousins and I were waiting our turn. I can remember being really hungry as I waited. Sometimes I'd nibble on a cold biscuit left over from breakfast.

By the time we kids were allowed to sit at the table, all the biscuits were stone cold. (Unfortunately, there always seemed to be plenty of spinach left in the bowl!)

When my uncles married, their wives let it be known that they felt this ritual was barbaric and the custom went away. Soon we kids were eating first, getting all the fluffy hot biscuits. I was never hungry after that...but mealtimes weren't as much fun.

—*Dot Ferguson, Hatfield Medina, Texas*

tea for two

Our parents owned and operated an upscale restaurant called Willard's on West Pico Boulevard in Beverly Hills from 1928 to 1959.

My younger sister, Wilda, and I were taught at a very early age to appreciate tasteful and attractive table settings, and we loved to get dressed up for our tea parties, which were part of a fun learning experience.

In this 1937 photo, I'm pouring a cup for Wilda. We were much too young to drink real tea at the time, but we did enjoy Kool-Aid served in an elegant manner!

—*LeeBerta Graham, Paso Robles, California*

oilcloth spread new life through the home

By Anne Fauvell, Rapid City, South Dakota

Most of our furniture and accessories were purchased on time payments back in the early 1940s. That included the kitchen table in our Brooklyn, New York, neighborhood.

In our Greenpoint cold-water flat, the table was the focal point for more than just meals. We did our homework, glued airplanes, built model cars and cut out paper-doll clothes there.

Of course, food was still a mainstay in our Italian family. We mixed meatballs and ground plum tomatoes for spaghetti sauce.

We always used an oilcloth on our wooden table with a blanket under the oilcloth to protect the wood from knife cuts.

One pattern of our kitchen oilcloth was red-and-white check, used during the fall and winter months. A flowered pattern was placed on the table during the spring and summer.

How rich we felt when a new oilcloth was placed on the table! No knife cuts, airplane-glue spots or spaghetti-sauce stains!

One drawback to a new oilcloth was the odor. As we ate our food, the aroma of oil, like heating oil, filled our nostrils.

How did we get rid of the new oilcloth odor? We rubbed garlic on the oilcloth to mask it. The garlic aroma permeated our kitchen and other four rooms for five months. But this was not a bother because our family loved garlic.

Usually, our oilcloth lasted six months. When the new oilcloth was placed on the table, bright and new, the old cloth was gently folded, then wrapped around our fig trees for the winter months so the bark would be protected from the cold, damp weather.

dining room became a salon on Sunday nights

Ed Sullivan and peanut butter diverted her attention while Mom curled her hair.

By Susan Bradley, Lancaster, California

Our dining room table was used as a gathering place for family meals, where manners were equally as important as the evening's supper. Each place setting had a knife and fork placed over a folded napkin, with a spoon nearby. Sitting with straight backs in our chairs and with napkins in our laps, my brother, sister and I never talked with food in our mouths or reached across the table for salt, pepper or a bowl of potatoes. But when Sunday evenings hit, these rules disappeared, thanks to my hair.

Mom allowed me to sit on our dining room table— a bastion of formality.

My hair was so straight it stuck out, which is what I call "petrified" straight. Although my mother straightened her hair, she actually had beautiful, naturally curly hair—a trait I didn't inherit!

After years of experimenting, Mom discovered that with the help of bobby pins, she could create curls in my hair. Because my mom was quite tall and needed me to be sitting at a comfortable height for her to work on my hair, she allowed me to sit on our dining room table—a bastion of formality. And to keep me still, she allowed me a second indulgence—a spoonful of peanut butter!

With anticipation, I turned and faced the television just as Ed Sullivan greeted us at 8 o'clock. With his unique way of talking, he would announce, while rubbing his hands together, "We have a really big show tonight, a really big show."

Hoping for a musical performance by Topo Gigio the mouse, I sat there on my family's dining room table for one solid hour, licking a tablespoon full of peanut butter and watching the show.

My grandmother, brother and sister were seated in the living room in front of the glowing television while my mother patiently pin-curled every single strand of hair on my 6-year-old head.

To this day, when I need to step on my dining room table (newspaper under foot, of course) to change a lightbulb or clean the ceiling fan, I look back fondly upon Sunday evenings spent with my family and I smile.

clearing the table
proved a windfall

An often-dreaded chore became a profitable adventure.

By Nancy Lebofsky, Tucson, Arizona

For much of the 1950s, my cousin, Jan, and I were the only children in an extended family of parents, maternal grandmother, great-aunts and great-uncles. As two little girls among so many adults, we received a lot of attention, especially at family gatherings.

All of those dinners were great, but the most memorable of them took place at our Great-Aunt Mae Taylor's apartment.

The old building where Aunt Mae and her brother, Irv, lived was narrow but deep.

There was a small kitchen in the rear, a bedroom in the middle and a living room overlooking the street.

The only way to seat all of us was to set up folding tables that ran the length of the living room. That meant carrying the dishes and food to and from the kitchen, through the bedroom, then squeezing between the living room furniture and the folding chairs that were set around the makeshift dining tables.

When it was time to clear the table for dessert, Uncle Irv had a surprise for Jan and me. He asked if we would help clear the table.

Handling the "good dishes" was quite a responsibility for two little girls, especially considering how far we had to carry them.

We began with Uncle Irv's setting. Imagine our surprise when several coins mysteriously appeared under each plate, cup and saucer. He told us the money was a reward for our help.

TIPSTERS. In 1952, Nancy Lebofsky (at left) posed with her cousin, Jan Sampson, and Uncle Irv and Aunt Mae.

As we carefully carried the dishes and coins back to the kitchen, the other relatives joined in. Soon every item we picked up from the table revealed a penny, nickel or dime. By the time the table was cleared, Jan and I shared quite a windfall.

Looking back on that day, I remember the surprise and delight Jan and I felt. I also recall the smiles and winks of the adults as they guided us toward the dishes that covered the hidden treasure.

And it was on that wonderful afternoon when we learned how even the youngest can contribute to the family.

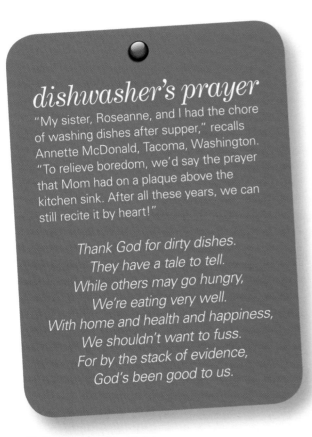

dishwasher's prayer

"My sister, Roseanne, and I had the chore of washing dishes after supper," recalls Annette McDonald, Tacoma, Washington. "To relieve boredom, we'd say the prayer that Mom had on a plaque above the kitchen sink. After all these years, we can still recite it by heart!"

Thank God for dirty dishes.
They have a tale to tell.
While others may go hungry,
We're eating very well.
With home and health and happiness,
We shouldn't want to fuss.
For by the stack of evidence,
God's been good to us.

colorful

Make the focal point of your home on the bright side!

carefree

as a summer day — adding zestful spice to every meal.

Virtue BROTHERS OF CALIFORNIA *chrome dinettes*

are the finest — both style-wise and quality-wise! Buy Virtue Dinettes and you have years of proud dining enjoyment ahead.

Chairs glide into place with the greatest of ease! Noiseless — Stainless — Smoothie Cushion Glides make the magic.

583/624
available with one or two extension leaves

VIRTUE BROS. MFG. CO.
5701 West Century Boulevard, Los Angeles 45, Calif.
Sold by leading department and furniture stores

Send to Dept. K for free color illustrated folder showing beautiful Virtue Bros. chrome dinettes

1953

clan coveted seats at 'Fat Gram's' table

Men and kids stayed out of the kitchen, while the women jockeyed for position. *By Margaret Dickson-Andrulonis, Pittsburgh, Pennsylvania*

I don't remember when Margaret Davis Wilson went from being my "Grandma" to being called "Fat Grandma," but that was how she was known to her 27 grandchildren and 32 great-grandchildren. Fortunately, she found the name a term of endearment.

Fat Gram was the queen of the family, and her throne was the old wooden kitchen table covered in a worn oilcloth.

Every Saturday, her children and their broods would descend upon Gram's small Victorian-style row house, where we all had our own places to congregate. The men took over the living room, and the kids went to Gram's bedroom to play. But the most cherished place for the ladies was at the kitchen table.

Because there were more people than seats, great pains were taken to ensure people didn't "shuffle their feet and lose their seat."

To avoid this, the moms would employ their kids to do the little tasks that weren't worth getting up for, such as fetching pops from the icebox or getting purses from the living room.

...her throne was the old wooden kitchen table...

When a mom had to use the restroom, one of her kids came and sat in the chair until she returned, giving them strict orders not to move. It was not unheard of for an aunt to bribe the child into giving up the chair! What a thrill for us kids to sit—albeit, temporarily—at Gram's table.

There, everything was discussed from family problems to neighborhood gossip. It was where everyone sampled Gram's fudge and potato salad...and where Gram signed and addressed the endless stream of grandchildren's birthday cards, each containing a dollar bill. The family gathered at the table to celebrate joyous occasions and to commiserate heartbreaking news, like Gram's passing in 1987.

I always yearned to be old enough to earn a reserved seat at Gram's table, but sadly, the table is gone. Thankfully, the wonderful memories live on.

the table was the heart of the home

Dad and Daughter Time

When I was a child in the early '40s, I looked forward to my daddy reading me the Sunday funnies. We sat at the dining room table while Mama prepared breakfast—percolated coffee for Daddy, hot cocoa for me and warm slices of cinnamon toast for all.

An additional treat, just on Sunday mornings, was a soft-boiled egg, served in a special egg cup, just the right size to hold one egg with the top half of the shell removed.

—*Faye Ann Bristol, Comstock Park, Michigan*

Quilting Bee Welcomed Baby

When my mother was "in the family way," her friends gathered around the dining table, making a quilt for her expected baby. Each one brought a scrap of material, put the blocks together and did hand quilting.

Early one morning, my dad called the doctor, who arrived before I left for school. All day, I sat on pins and needles, wondering what was happening at home.

As soon as school was out, I ran home the full three-fourths of a mile and burst breathlessly into the house, and there was the beautiful quilt draped cozily over a basket and covering a mound with a fluff of pinkish red hair—my new sister!

—*Betty Ann Baker Temple, Bellevue, Nebraska*

Like a Dream

In the '30s, my mother and her sister spent many nights with their aunts and uncles at their family home. Often, in the middle of the night, they were awakened and invited to join the group in the kitchen "for a little bite."

They found the entire O'Brien family gathered around the table, enjoying toast and scrambled eggs, telling wonderful stories that delighted the two little girls. I treasure this happy handed-down memory.

—*Charlotte Phillips, Winchester, Kentucky*

If people were not meant to have midnight snacks, why do they put a light in the refrigerator?

peas, peas go away!

She thought she had a leg up on the pea problem in 1946, until her mother caught wind of her scheme.

By Mary Morrison, Fairfax, California

When I was 6 and my brother Bobby about 5, in 1946, we had to eat our vegetables. Corn and string beans were OK, and even carrots were tolerated. It was the peas that made life unbearable in our Yonkers, New York, home. They appeared on the menu once a week, or if we were unlucky, twice—in the additional form of peas and carrots.

Mom was a kind woman, not too strict, but she was going to see that we ate right—or at least ate all the common vegetables.

It seemed to take hours to force down those peas, one by one, chewing and grinding each one to oblivion. They caught in my throat, they tasted terrible, I complained.

"They're good for you and you can't have dessert until you finish those peas," was the standard reply.

Once, while I chewed, my hands rubbed the tabletop. They felt the smooth, cool Formica and traced the beautiful swirls.

My fingers touched the wide band of chrome encircling the oval tabletop and discovered that the bent tubular chrome legs were hollow where they were welded to the top.

Pea Didn't Make a Sound

I made my face blank and looked up at my mother working in the kitchen. As I kept watching her, I slipped my hand to my plate, stole a pea and slowly, carefully brought it back to the opening in the leg.

I put the pea at the edge, and it was a second or so before I had the courage to let go. I held my breath, my eyes fixed on my mother's back, but the pea fell the entire length of the leg and didn't make a sound. The other peas on my plate quickly followed. I asked to be excused and fetched my Popsicle as my brother was still staring at his plate of peas.

"You finished your peas so quickly tonight," Mom said. "I think I've begun to like them," I lied.

Later, I shared my discovery with Bobby. The next time we had peas, we looked across the table at each other, eyes acknowledging, but faces straight.

Tired of waiting for us to finish the peas, Mom got up to do the dishes. My brother giggled as his first pea slid down the tube, and I shot him a dirty glance.

The game continued for weeks, and Mother was impressed at how we had grown to like our peas.

Then one day she said, "Do you smell something funny, Mary?"

Couldn't Hide the Smell

I froze. It never occurred to me the peas might rot in their hiding place in the table legs.

"I don't smell anything, Mom," I said quickly. But when I sniffed, I smelled it, too.

Later when we were alone, Bobby and I plotted how we could get the peas out. One morning, we struggled to lift and turn over the heavy table. Working hard as my brother's face turned red, we were able to move the table about two inches but couldn't lift it. I thought Bobby was going to cry.

A few days later, Mom sat at the table with Bobby and me as we ate.

"You know," she said, "I tried to find out what was making that rotten odor. I cleaned the kitchen 20 times."

My head remained bowed over the plate of peas, not even stealing a look at my brother.

"The smell was strongest by the table, so I got your father to help me turn it over. We found peas...in the legs of the table. How do you think they got there?" she asked.

"It was Mary's idea," Bobby blurted out.

"Mary, you should know better. Don't you think I should be angry?"

"I'm sorry, Mom," I said.

"Do you understand that it was wrong?"

"Yes," I said, waiting for the inevitable.

"Well, perhaps I should not have forced you to eat those peas." I couldn't believe my ears.

"In the future, I won't make you eat any vegetables you really don't want to eat," she said.

I volunteered to clean up the kitchen to make up for the mess in the legs, and clean out the legs, too.

As I grew up, I came to love exotic vegetables—cauliflower, zucchini, asparagus, eggplant. But after all these years, I still hate to eat peas.

kids went to great lengths to avoid foods

Sprouting Liver Plants

When I was a busy mom in the '50s, every Wednesday was fried-calves'-liver-smothered-in-onions day. On Wednesdays, Dad and I had quality time, while the children took their dinners and ate in their little red clubhouse in the backyard.

Twenty years later, one of the children revealed that what they were really doing in the clubhouse was burying their liver slices. Whenever I need a good laugh, I look out back and imagine "liver plants" sprouting in the garden.

—*Rochelle Smith, Charleston, South Carolina*

Sis Took Rasher Measures

Every Sunday after church, Mother prepared a big breakfast of bacon, eggs and pancakes. We kids weren't allowed to leave the table until we finished everything on our plates.

One of my sisters hated bacon, so one Sunday morning she hid hers under the big white collar on her dress. As soon as Mother's back was turned, my sister got up and stood on the floor vent, pretending to warm up. She then disposed of the bacon through one of the large spaces in the vent.

Lucky for her, Mother never figured out why the aroma of bacon lingered so long in our house.

—*Martha Mahon, Trenton, New Jersey*

Discovery Didn't Register with Dad

Like so many kids, I hated peas when I was growing up. Since we didn't have a pet and Mother always said we had to finish everything on our plate, I had to come up with a way to make those peas disappear.

Next to my chair at the kitchen table was a heating register, which I thought was just perfect for those little peas! Not only did I get rid of that detested vegetable, no one was any wiser.

Then one day many years later, my father needed to put in a new furnace. While taking down some pipes, countless green little balls fell out of the pipe that came from the kitchen. He just couldn't figure it out and had to tell me and my sons the story. I burst out laughing. After all this time, my secret was out!

—*Eileen Mercea, McKeesport, Pennsylvania*

Breakfast Bugged Brother

In 1928, Mom used cornmeal to make a hot morning cereal for us children, and she dressed it up by adding some large Sultana raisins.

When we finished eating, she asked us how we liked our new cereal. My youngest brother, Bob, who was about 5, said he liked the cereal but didn't like the bugs...all his raisins were neatly tucked under the edge of his cereal bowl.

—*Murray Edwards, Victoria, British Columbia*

charlotte russe was just desserts

Excitement over rare treat overwhelmed him.

By Stan Drescher, Suffern, New York

Hoch's Candy Store was the neighborhood sweet shop when I was growing up in New York City in 1935. One bitter cold day in the dead of winter, Mr. Hoch obtained an unusual buy—12 charlotte russes! Naturally, he displayed them in the front glass case.

The charlotte russe was a unique treat made with sponge cake and a dollop of whipped cream. The cream was twisted into the shape of a mountain and placed on top of a square cake. Together, they were set into a small white paper cup with a

> *Six eyes stared at this rarest of all desserts. Never had we encountered a treasure like this!*

false bottom. The top rim of the paper had a spiked border and looked like a crown, befitting this royal treat.

The whipped cream was real, made with heavy cream and powdered sugar. Nothing was as great or could top it, except a maraschino cherry, and it did.

Papa and Mr. Hoch were friends; they belonged to the same synagogue. He convinced my father to take the remaining three for 3 cents, especially after he added, "You'll pay me next time."

Papa had never bought anything so frivolous before. He spent long hours as a tailor and made $9 a week. He also earned fees and tips saying prayers at Long Island cemeteries. Mama did all the buying, shopping and cooking.

Dessert wasn't a common thing in our home. During dinner, Mama set the three charlotte russes on the table—one in front of each of us three brothers, Jake, Morty and me. Six eyes stared at this rarest of all desserts. Never had we encountered a treasure like this!

Jake and Morty started to gulp their food. Because I was younger, I couldn't keep up or contain myself.

Before anyone else could finish, I grabbed my charlotte russe—but greed, fate and disaster each played a role. My fingers didn't grasp the tissue-thin paper cup, and it went flying from the table. In slow motion, just like in the movies, I saw this treasure fall upside down on the damp newspapers that protected Mama's clean floor!

Immediately the false bottom gave way, and the cake, whipped cream and cherry splattered onto the newsprint! My life was over. Mama sympathized; Jack and Morty just laughed.

Today when I'm dining out and want dessert, I choose rice pudding. The charlotte russe remains in the annals of history, although it conjures up the feelings, thoughts of my father and excitement that preceded the upside-down world of a 4-year-old on that fateful day.

a desire for doughnuts led to chuckles

By Joe Juntunen, Carlton, Minnesota

Laughter was always a part of my childhood, but my most memorable moment involved Mrs. Anderson, Mama's friend. She was a large woman with an appetite to match. After eating a delicacy, she'd always say, "Oh, I mustn't do this. I'm ruining my diet."

One day before Mrs. Anderson's next visit, Mama decided my sister Elsa and I would sit with the women at the dining room table. Elsa and I never laughed. Plus, Mama did not have enough doughnuts for everyone. If there were any left over, the kids in the kitchen could share them.

True to form later that day, Mrs. Anderson ate a doughnut and announced, "If I eat one more, I think I'll positively explode."

Unexpectedly, Elsa and I burst out laughing. And then it happened. Thinking Mama and Mrs. Anderson had retired to the living room, our brother Dennis shouted from the kitchen, "Did the fat lady eat all the doughnuts?"

I put my face in my napkin and soon was laughing so hard that I thought the whole room was shaking. My eyes were watering and my stomach hurt.

When I looked across the top of my napkin, I saw Elsa laughing, too. To hide her giggle, she tried to put her face behind the curtains. In doing so, she pulled them off the rods and they fell on the floor. Mama's world came crashing down along with them.

I don't remember how Mrs. Anderson reacted to our outbursts, but after she left, Mama started scolding us...until before she herself couldn't resist and started laughing, too.

FUN FAMILY. Joe Juntunen and his family caught a case of the giggles during one family friend's visit. This 1953 photo shows Joe (back row, third from the right) with his parents and 12 siblings.

laughter was the main course

Heel Was Hard to Pass Up

When I was growing up in the '40s, Dad used to cook spaghetti sauce and meatballs on Monday nights. Guests were always welcome, and many came.

Since Dad didn't like white bread, he served a large loaf of pumpernickel with the meal. The moment it was sliced, someone would grab the heel, the most coveted piece. Then a chase began!

The heel was passed from person to person, and when we finally sat down to eat, the lucky "winner" ceremoniously lavished butter on it and slowly enjoyed each bite—much to the envy of all the rest of us.

—*Bonnie Everett, Grants Pass, Oregon*

lunchtime laughs

Our mother was working in 1953, so my sister and I were in charge of fixing lunch. We usually served tomato soup and crackers.

Dad didn't allow silliness at the table, but one day, in the midst of giggles, my little brother leaned his head back in laughter and brought his face back down, right into his tomato soup! Dad couldn't help himself...he joined us in a great round of laughter we'll never forget.

—*Dorothy Hart*
Kokomo, Indiana

Do Drop in

We had a drop-leaf table, which had been extended for a special occasion. We were all seated around the table, and the meal had been served, when the drop leaf dropped, right into the lap of the guest of honor! After our initial shock, we all came down with contagious laughter.

—*Valerie Webb*
Santa Monica, California

Sharing the Chicken

Back in 1900, when my father was 8 years old, the only piece of chicken he would ever eat was the breast.

One Sunday, his parents invited the local parson for their usual chicken dinner. As my father looked on anxiously, the parson got first choice from the platter. He took the breast, and my father said aloud, "I knew he'd get it!" Dad was promptly excused from the table.

—*Charles Terry*
Elgin, Illinois

1951

cupid had lunch at woolworth's

Their meeting at a five-and-ten was priceless.

By Doris DeVault Bacon, Globe, Arizona

After my aunt, Edith Bitzer, became widowed in 1947, she invited me, then 19, to visit her friends, Martin and Marion Mortensen, in Phoenix, Arizona.

We arrived in Phoenix on December 7. Before our planned returned, Aunt Edith's father, my grandfather, became ill and she went back home to New Jersey to care for him.

The Mortensens invited me to stay. They became my Arizona "parents" and their daughter, Lois, my good friend. As long as I was staying for a while, I decided to look for work. I didn't know then that this decision would lead to my staying in Arizona permanently.

I had worked for White's 5-and-10-cent store in Paulsboro, New Jersey, so I headed for the Woolworth's on Washington and First Streets in Phoenix. I was hired to work in the notion department. After Christmas, I was transferred to the lunch counter.

While I was working at the lunch counter, I met Ed Bacon, a tall and handsome fella who worked around the corner at Brown's Boots and Saddles. Soon after we met, Ed asked me to the

DOING THE TOWN. Ed and Doris (above left) were coming out of the Fox Theatre in Phoenix in 1948 when this photo was snapped. At left is one of their love notes written on a Woolworth's napkin.

> Love is the most important ingredient in any dish.

local policeman's ball. But I didn't feel I knew enough about this cowboy to go out with him just yet.

Ed and I continued to meet at the lunch counter, where we became better acquainted by talking and writing notes to each other on paper napkins.

By then I had learned from my boss that Ed

I was too much in love to consider a future at Woolworth's.

was a perfect gentleman, so the next time Ed asked me out, I eagerly accepted.

It was a good thing I accepted on the second offer. Ed told me later that he didn't make a habit of asking a girl out the second time after he'd been turned down.

Even though my boss had convinced me Ed was a good guy, he was beginning to become concerned about how much time I was spending with Ed.

My boss had planned to move me into management at the store. But he must have seen the handwriting on the wall, or maybe the handwriting on his napkins, and he realized

that I was too much in love to consider a future at Woolworth's.

One night in August 1948, Ed was at the Mortensens' for a family birthday party. He pulled me aside and said, "Let's get married, tonight."

Ed said he had told his mother that he was going to ask me and that if I said yes, he would come back home to get her.

I told Ed I couldn't possibly get married that night. I would have to shop for something to wear, and we'd have to buy the rings.

All that did was postpone the inevitable for a day.

The next morning, I called my parents back in Paulsboro and told them about the wedding. Then I went out and bought a suit. We got our license, bought rings and were married!

We've had a great life together, and it all began at the Woolworth's lunch counter. In my box of treasures, I still have the napkin notes that started our romance.

Ed often tells me that he found a million-dollar baby in a 5-and-10 store!

Now's the time for

Can you think of a more appropriate dish for moments like these than a delicious, festive Jell-O gelatin dessert? We ask you.

JELL-O IS A REGISTERED TRADE-MARK OF GENERAL FOODS CORPORATION   Copr. 1953, General Foods Corporation

JELL-O
BRAND
GELATIN DESSERT
SIX DELICIOUS FLAVORS

1953

JEFFERY HODACH

cooking up romance

For these couples, the way to the heart was through the stomach.

Proof Was in the Pudding

In 1945, I saw a handsome sailor in church and convinced my brother to set us up. We had our first date on June 14, and by September, we knew we were meant to be together.

That Christmas, we gathered around the table of Bob's family for a traditional Swedish feast, consisting of 12 delicious courses.

The dessert was rice pudding, with a lone almond inside. Whoever got the almond in their serving would be married next. Well, of course, they planted the almond in my dish.

After my embarrassment passed, Bob and I proudly announced our wedding for the following June. I'll never forget that loving memory being surrounded by loved ones...and the man of my dreams.

—*Hilda Sand, Canton, Connecticut*

Kneed Out of Spinsterhood

I was determined to be a spinster teacher when I completed my associate's degree in education in 1961 at age 19. I was raised on a Minnesota farm in a family of 12 children, with seven brothers, and had had quite enough of the male gender.

I received a teaching contract in Miles City, Montana. Teaching took most of my time, but I did date a few very polite men. They did not, however, change my determination to remain a dedicated full-time teacher.

My roommate was dating one of the few male teachers, Bob While, and had him over for dinner. Our table was small, but when I felt his knee touching mine, I knew it was not an accident.

I was flabbergasted and began blushing from head to toe. When I glared at Bob, he responded with a wink!

I quickly excused myself from the table. But that was how it all began.

Bob soon stopped seeing my roommate, and we dated for six months before marrying in July 1962.

—*Dianne While, Gillette, Wyoming*

It Pays to Share

I was working on a telephone company line crew in Le Roy, Illinois, in 1948. We ate our meals in a popular local cafe called the Lee.

A pretty girl named Judy Dooley also ate lunch there and always had a piece of chocolate pie. I just had to meet her, so I devised a plan.

One noon our crew got to the restaurant early, where I promptly bought all of the chocolate pie. Then I told the waitress that when Judy ordered her pie, she was to say I had the last piece but would be happy to share.

That got us properly introduced, and we were married 18 months later. We still enjoy, and share, chocolate pie.

—*Robert Brubaker, Dade City, Florida*

Home-Cooked Meal Sealed the Deal

I taught in a school 12 miles from my home, so on PTA meeting nights, I stayed in town for dinner. One time, the school secretary invited me to her house for a home-cooked meal instead of my usual dining out.

She served lettuce and tomato salad, round steak with gravy and mushrooms, mashed potatoes and baby peas. Dessert was peach cobbler a la mode.

Ever since that night, it's been my favorite meal. I fell in love with the cook and married her!

—*Alvin Anderson, Claremont, California*

Sandwich Saved the Day

In 1948, I was invited by friends to spend a weekend at their rustic cabin in the Indiana dunes. Everyone had to carry in their own provisions and prepare their own meals.

On the third day, all of my friends had to leave. But I decided to stay for the rest of the day on my own.

That morning, a girl arrived at the cabin. She was pretty as a picture, and I quickly made the acquaintance of Patricia Durkin.

During the day, I realized that I had no supplies, as my friends had not prepared for a third day. The nearest store was a 1½-mile walk through the woods.

When I mentioned the problem to Pat, she said she had brought along a large roast beef sandwich that she would be glad to share.

Pat and I dated for a year, then became engaged. A year later, we were married. On the second week of our honeymoon, Pat got the mumps. *That* we did not share.

—*Edward Peschel*
Chicago, Illinois

mom's kitchen was the place to be

Whether it was a special occasion like my sister's graduation party in the '40s (above) or just dropping by for a taste of her delicious minestrone soup, we always gathered in the kitchen when we visited my mom, Theresa Bianchi. Whenever Mom (standing second from left) laughed, the joy inside her turned her face beet red!

—Mary Compagnoni, Buffalo, New York

CHAPTER TWO

Memorable Mealtimes

Down-home breakfasts on the farm...leisurely lunches around the kitchen table...Sunday suppers at Grandma's. The most enjoyable times at the table showcased a selection of flavorful foods as well friends and family to share them with.

"Foremost among memories of my grandma are her elegant Sunday dinners," shares Donna Kindberg-Perron of Bridgewater, Massachusetts. "The moment we entered her house, we were greeted with the aroma of a roast cooking in the oven.

"The menu didn't vary much...mashed potatoes, fresh vegetables and gravy. Because it was Sunday, Grandma was dressed in her best clothes, protected by a freshly starched apron.

"She set the table with fine linen and her best china. Minutes before we came to the table, Grandpa was already at the head of the table, patiently waiting to carve the roast."

Makes the mouth water just thinking about it. More soul-stirring recollections are on the menu in this chapter...

waking up to memorable
summer sundays

By Louise Nelson
Waynesville, North Carolina

On Sundays in the summertime on our North Carolina tenant farm, the roosters woke us to the aroma of breakfast cooking on the woodstove.

By the time we'd washed our hands and faces, Mama and Grandmother had a big breakfast ready. It had to be big—there were 13 of us living in the house.

This was around the early '30s. After my father died, we moved in with Grandfather and Grandmother. Our family numbered seven, and there were already six in my grandparents' home in Haywood County.

We were poor in those Depression years. There was no electricity or indoor plumbing...water had to be carried and wood cut for the stove. Even so, Mama and Grandma sure could cook!

Breakfast was usually ham, sausage or streaked meat with eggs, gravy, buttermilk biscuits, butter, jelly, coffee and milk.

If the hens weren't laying and we were out of ham and sausage, there'd be creamed corn, applesauce, biscuits and fried mountain trout with grits. Often there was oatmeal, which Grandpa said would "stick to our ribs."

Hurried for Church

We girls hurried to do the breakfast dishes, then made our beds and dressed for church in our Sunday slippers and best dresses. We'd already taken our baths on Saturday night in the washtub in the kitchen, but we had to brush our teeth and hang our toothbrushes back up on the wall.

While we were getting ready, Grandpa would check on the livestock and feed the hogs. Meanwhile, Mama milked the cows and Grandma killed chickens for dinner.

Mama (who still had small children) and Grandma stayed home to prepare the big meal. The little ones were too hard to manage on the long walk, so it was up to Grandpa to get the rest of us to church.

When he announced, "It's time to go to

BAREFOOT DAYS.
Who needed shoes in summer in the '30s? Louise Nelson (center) posed with sisters Ethel, Ruth, Beatrice and Mazie in their flour sack dresses.

the meetinghouse," we began the four-mile trek from the farm in Big Branch to the Crabtree Baptist Church, walking through pastures and along the edges of corn and tobacco fields.

We enjoyed Sunday school and the church service but lost no time getting back home to that special Sunday dinner.

Mama and Grandma usually made fried chicken or chicken and dumplings,

We were poor in those Depression years. There was no electricity or indoor plumbing...water had to be carried and wood cut for the stove. Even so, Mama and Grandma sure could cook!

plus biscuits and corn bread. There might also be roast turkey, backbones and ribs. Vegetables came fresh from the garden— green beans, new potatoes, tomatoes, cucumbers and other greens.

For dessert, there was often a cake, pie or cobbler made with fresh strawberries, blackberries or dewberries.

Second-Shift Seating

Sunday was the big day when aunts, uncles and cousins came to visit, so the house was full. We kids had to wait for the second table before we could eat.

The girls did the dishes afterward, but we made fast work of it so we could go out and play Annie over, hide-and-seek, hopscotch and other games with our

cousins. The boys played marbles, baseball or horseshoes...or sometimes went down to the creek bank to fish.

Adults gathered on the porch or under the shade trees to talk about crops or gardens or canning. The men would often show off any new pigs or calves.

We'd take our cousins to a special place where we could hear our echo. We'd holler, "Hello over there," and the echo would come back from the other side of the mountain.

By 5 o'clock, we were gathered back in the kitchen for a supper of leftovers. Then the relatives started to head home.

Now our family would settle on the porch until bedtime. We'd listen to the outdoor sounds and watch the chickens go to roost in the tall trees, and the kids would try to catch lightning bugs.

Everyone would tell what the other families had talked about while enjoying the cool of the night. Those are such wonderful days to remember.

Family—a group of people, no two of whom like their eggs cooked the same way.

cereal was a standby

NO COOKING REQUIRED. "In 1954, when my brother Jack Vance and his family came for a visit to our home in Bazine, Kansas, I heard children's voices in the kitchen one morning," recalls Vera Wilkins of Claflin. "Grabbing my camera, I found my 11-year-old son, Don, fixing breakfast for my daughter, Carol (far left), my niece Janice and my 2-year-old nephew Joe, with his play gun on the table. Sugar Jets was a new cereal at that time."

BREAKFAST IN A BOX. "What a classic 1961 breakfast shot this is!" remarks Katherine Dowling of Louisville, Colorado. "From left are my cousin Lela, age 4; my younger brother Matt, 3; my cousin Richard, 6; me, nicknamed 'Trinkie,' age 6; and my sister, Liz, 5.

Those milk bottles were delivered to our house in Falls Church, Virginia. I love the place mats, the radio on the windowsill and the Wheaties and Alpha-Bits boxes. And the dining room table is still in the family."

SNAP, CRACKLE AND A BIT OF POP. "This is our son, Dave, in June 1959, when he was almost 2," says Betty Pettit of State College, Pennsylvania. "Dave is eating breakfast while wearing one of the old hats of his dad, Bill. To this day, Dave can usually be seen wearing a hat, but now they are his own. The slide was taken in our home when we lived in Lancaster."

pancakes sweetened their love

Grandpa's love letters to Grandma included a special surprise.

By Karen Mitzel, Luseland, Saskatchewan

Grandpa always made my grandma pancakes on their anniversary. It doesn't sound very romantic, but, in fact, it was the sweetest gift.

Grandma and Grandpa were married on a hot, dusty August afternoon in 1937. They'd planned to wed after the harvest, but since the crops had shriveled in the long drought, there was no harvest and they decided not to wait.

The large farm kitchen table was set with a ragtag assortment of cutlery and china, most of which had been borrowed from kind neighbors.

After the reception, gifts were opened. Most were homemade and inexpensive. However, the smallest package drew the most gasps. It contained two one-way tickets to Vancouver. My grandma and grandpa squealed with delight.

There was nothing for them in the drought-stricken prairies, and they had wanted to try their luck on Canada's west coast. The only thing stopping them was a shortage of money for the trip. Now, thanks to wealthy Uncle Ernie, they were going to Vancouver.

Once there, they rented a room in a boardinghouse. Grandpa immediately searched for work and found a job in the logging industry. But it was 200 miles up the coast. Grandma was now left alone in a big, strange city with no money.

At the logging camp, Grandpa grew worried about Grandma. So one morning, while surrounded by the huge amount of food available at the logging camp, Grandpa placed four pancakes in a clean hanky and mailed them to Grandma.

Flapjacks by Mail

When Grandma received the pancakes more than a week later, she got a whiff of the food before opening the package. Instead of the tantalizing aroma of hot flapjacks, though, it was a rotting moldy odor.

Inside was a note, slightly soggy and stained, that read, "For you, my precious love. I will continue to send food until I return to your side. Love, Jack." That was the first of many pancake parcels.

After a few months, Grandpa found work near Vancouver, and he and Grandma were together again. Grandma never forgot Grandpa's thoughtfulness, and every time pancakes were made in their home, wonderful memories were served along with them.

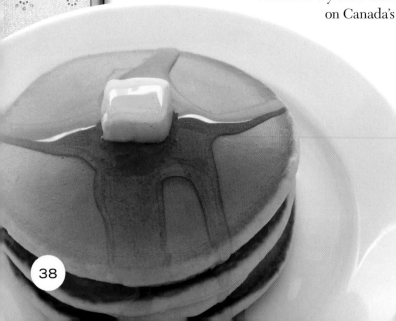

Around the Table

"My daughter, Hailey, learned this prayer at school. Her great-grandfather likes her to say it before Sunday dinners," notes Michelle Foutty of Madison Heights, Virginia.

We thank You, God, in Heaven, for all Your love and care that You have given to us at home and everywhere. For many years, You kept us at sleep, at work and play. Oh, dear God, love and care for us today and every day. Amen.

Early-Day Dining Made a Difference

In the good old days, families made a point of sitting down to breakfast before starting a busy day at school or work. That's what the Krueger family was doing on this morning in 1947.

Don Krueger of Delafield, Wisconsin, shared this classic morning scene taken when the family lived in nearby Wauwatosa. (From left to right are Don, Niel, Marianne, Lyle and Mom Florence.)

Seventeen at the time, Don—who admits he liked to pour chocolate milk on his cereal in his youth—was too busy digging into his bowl to look at his dad snapping the photo.

1950

breakfast was slow & savored

People took time for the most important meal of the day.

Breakfast Bribery

On school days, Mama encouraged us five children to eat a good breakfast. "It will help you think better as you do your lessons," she often said.

One time she ordered some special cereal bowls for her two youngest…my sister, Helen, and me. There were pictures at the bottom of the bowl, but you couldn't see the entire picture unless you ate all your cereal.

Then she purchased some blue glass Shirley Temple bowls for us. Shredded wheat biscuits or homemade bread broken into bits, sprinkled with sugar and covered with rich milk from our cow, "Tiddlywinks," were favorite treats eaten out of these bowls. And, when we finished, there was Shirley's smiling face.

To this day, breakfast is my favorite meal.

—*Mildred Geraldson Ashley*
Endicott, New York

Granddad Jammed

When my grandparents hosted their six grandchildren for vacation or holidays in Thorndale, Texas, in the mid-'40s, my granddad always prepared our breakfast.

He put a large chunk of freshly churned butter into a hot iron skillet, placed a slice of bread on top and fried it to a golden brown.

He kept turning out fried toast with homemade plum jam as long as there were "customers" to eat it. —*Carroll Wilson*
Olney, Texas

Sunday Morning Ritual

During the '50s, when I was growing up in Milwaukee, Wisconsin, our ritual on Sunday mornings after church was to stop at a local bakery for ham and rolls.

If our timing was right, we could get to the counter just as the baker was bringing out a basket of hot rolls. The thinly sliced ham stayed warm wrapped in foil, still in its natural juices.

We purchased a pound of delicious homemade German potato salad, and brunch was complete.
—*Fred Kurtz*
De Soto, Wisconsin

Poached Eggs Deluxe

I looked forward to visiting my grandparents in the '40s and '50s.

Grandma often served poached eggs for breakfast. I didn't like my eggs poached, so I smothered them with fried potatoes and the delicious chili sauce she made with vegetables from Grandpa's garden.

Add to that her fluffy homemade bread and preserves, and breakfast was such a treat, I didn't mind the eggs at all! —*Nan Hale*
West Valley City, Utah

the lunch hour was a time of leisure

Food wasn't fast and family came first.

By Jeannette Hagerty, Walla Walla, Washington

Back in the 1940s, the sequence of each day's meals was breakfast, dinner and supper, with the noon dinner being the main meal.

That was no different in Pocatello, Idaho, a railroad town where I grew up. When the whistle at the railyard blew at 12 o'clock, it was time to head home.

The schools closed, and only those children who were bussed in from surrounding farms stayed to eat their sack lunches.

Many businesses shut their doors, and those remaining open were manned by skeleton crews. Unlike today, few people shopped during lunchtime.

After walking home from school and work, we four kids and Dad would be welcomed by Mother and the aromas of a wonderful meal waiting for us.

Flanked by windows on one side, our dining room was a cheerful place, where Mother covered the Queen Anne-style table with a freshly ironed, flowered tablecloth and set out pretty dishes and silverware.

We always sat at the same place, with Dad and all the food at the head. It was his job to fill the plates according to each person's wishes. Roast chicken...round steak...fresh vegetables...tender potatoes...pudding. What a mouthwatering selection my dear Mother always prepared!

Mother was a stickler for proper etiquette and often quoted Emily Post. My dad teased her and continued with his own unacceptable eating practices of wolfing down his food and using a "boardinghouse reach" to pass the platters. We kids tended to copy him...much to Mother's consternation.

Between bites, we would play guessing games or tell of interesting things that had happened that morning.

Too quickly, the clock ticked closer to 1 o'clock. The kids had to head back to school, and Dad needed to return to work. But we took comfort in knowing tomorrow would offer the same warm memories and down-home dinners.

> *Flanked by windows on one side, our dining room was a cheerful place, where Mother covered the Queen Anne-style table with a freshly ironed, flowered tablecloth and set out pretty dishes and silverware.*

Around the Table

They Served Lunch with Love

These 1956 lunchroom ladies (left) in Jamesville, North Carolina, were so treasured by the students, they honored them with this photo in their yearbook that year. From left to right are Effie Mizelle, Sally Gaines and Chessie Beck, my husband's grandmother.

—*Lois Beck, Williamston, North Carolina*

Baked Potato Lunches Were Best

During World War II, when everyone in our small community in Nebraska was growing a victory garden, my parents planted the entire lot next to our house—most of it in potatoes.

My three brothers and I had to pick the bugs off those growing plants. The grief of this chore was forgotten after school began, though, because we knew when we went home for lunch, we would sometimes find a big baked potato waiting for us, topped with lots of butter and slices of sweet onions.

—*Janice Fluegel, Amarillo, Texas*

Al Fresco Fare

Our lunch in Seattle, Washington, in 1948 featured real glassware and plates. We also got real milk to drink, as can be seen from our milk mustaches (below).

My friends Susan and Patty and I (center) were sitting at a just-the-right-size table made by my grandfather George Lund in his carpentry shop. To this day, I can smell the piles of wood shavings.

—*Carol Juhlin, Seattle, Washington*

Chow Time

When I was a teen in the '30s, I delivered the Sunday paper in Ogdensburg, New York. As a reward for establishing new customers, the newspaper treated us to a lunch observing the New York National Guard on maneuvers.

I'm the first in line in this photo (above). Little did I know that this would be the first of many chow lines I would stand in. When I was 18, I was drafted into the Army Air Corps.

—*Ronald McDonald Massena, New York*

43

1950

simple sandwiches always satisfied

Lunches didn't have to be big to take a bite out of hunger.

Bad Choice

My uncle, Clifford Taggart, and his sister Dolores didn't have the same taste in sandwiches when they attended a country school in Fulton Township, Iowa. Dolores packed the sandwiches and used her favorite filling—half a large green pepper, flattened out. From the look on Uncle Clifford's face (right), this was not to his liking.

—*Janet Van Eps, Edgewater, Colorado*

Lunch Included...No Bologna!

Many years ago, I was working for a local farmer who was paying the unheard price of 5 cents a box to pick strawberries.

A bunch of us kids signed on and picked awhile, but it was a hot day and we all got hungry.

The farmer's wife called us in for lunch, and she brought out a big platter of hot bologna sandwiches on homemade brown bread. I still think of them. —*Walter Grist, Westville, Nova Scotia*

Tempted by Tomatoes

When I was growing up in Kansas City during World War II, everyone grew a victory garden for the war effort. We only had corn and string beans, but Mrs. Giamavio, next door, grew a larger garden half planted with delicious yellow pear-shaped tomatoes. Soon I was under the fence helping myself to these small bites.

When I was on my way home from school one day, Mrs. Giamavio called me in and asked if I would like a sandwich. She made me a peanut butter sandwich with the most delicious tomato preserves I had ever tasted.

When I thanked her, she said she would give me a jar of her preserves—if I would stop taking her tomatoes. I filled in the hole under the fence the next day.

—*Chuck Allen, Kansas City, Missouri*

Vegetarian Delight Was Ahead of Its Time

I grew up in Ambridge, Pennsylvania, north of Pittsburgh. During the height of rationing in the 1940s, my father grew plenty of green peppers, tomatoes and yellow onions.

Mom would saute the onions, add the green peppers and tomatoes and cook until they were all tender. After dipping Mom's homemade bread in the sauce, we mounded up the peppers, tomatoes and onions on the bread. Delicious!

—*Jean Vogel, Annandale, Virginia*

Man cannot live by bread alone...he needs peanut butter and jelly to go with it.

from scratch for the boys in service

A little taste of home meant the world to those in uniform.

Her Cookies Passed the Censor

I wrote to my wife, Esther, almost daily during World War II when I was a master sergeant assigned to Gen. Eisenhower's American headquarters. Esther made great cookies, and everyone looked forward to my getting a package of them in the mail.

The censor, Warrant Officer Clinch, and I became good friends. I guess he got tired of reading all my letters home, so one day he said, "Carl, I know that you know what you can put in a letter and what you can't. So if you will just leave the envelopes unsealed, I will seal them and write 'censored' across the flap and sign them without reading them."

That was fine with me, and I was grateful for his kindness. But WO Clinch had another reason, I soon discovered.

Esther wrote that she sometimes found notes in my letters that usually read something like, "Dearest Esther. We all love you madly. Please send more cookies." The notes were signed, "The Censor."

—*Carl Nelson, Whittier, California*

Feast Fit for a King

While I was in the Air Force in the '50s, stationed in Arkansas, I asked for a three-day pass so that I could visit my Great-Aunt Hattie.

The first morning I was there, Aunt Hattie asked me what I wanted to eat. "Steak, chicken, you name it—I'll fix you anything."

I said, "OK, I want a mess of black-eyed peas, white onions, corn bread and a tall glass of milk."

She was aghast, but to me, a Southerner, this was a meal the Air Force cooks wouldn't know how to fix. She was delighted, and I left with a memory of a meal fit for a king.

—*Philip Keil, San Antonio, Texas*

Pasta Across the Pacific

My brother-in-law, Vincent D'Onofrio, was a radioman with the 25th Signal Co. in Korea in 1953 and '54. His wife (my sister Sara) and I wanted to do something special for Vincent and his buddies, so we decided to send them spaghetti and meatballs.

With Mom's help, we cooked batches of sauce with meatballs and canned it in jars. Then we packed up boxes of spaghetti and grated cheese, all well-wrapped to prevent breakage during the long trip.

We even hollowed out a large loaf of Italian bread and hid a bottle of wine inside. That was carefully wrapped, too.

Everything arrived in Korea in tip-top shape, Vincent told us later. After finding a portable burner to cook on, he and his buddies ate a home-cooked Italian meal out of their mess kits. Knowing they enjoyed the treat made our hours of cooking worthwhile. It felt great!

—*Josephine Rachiele, West Babylon, New York*

Hotcakes on the Home Front

Winning World War II on the home front meant keeping the boys in the service healthy and happy. USO centers like this one in Fall River, Massachusetts (above), which was near a large naval base in Newport, Rhode Island, accomplished that purpose.

Eileen O'Grady of Petersham, Massachusetts, found this great photo while cleaning out an aunt's house, noting, "I was just a kid of 7 or 8 years old when this was taken, in about 1942, but I remember those times well."

Eileen's Aunt Catherine Sullivan is at the stove, just to the left of the coffeepots, making pancakes. None of the other ladies could be identified, "but they're all involved in the war effort by keeping the sailors happy and well fed," says Eileen.

"I think the picture speaks a lot about the era. Notice the lady on the far left in the lovely black dress, hat and apron and holding the box of Sunnyfield pancake mix. It was probably Sunday morning, and she'd been to church. I love all of the ladies' aprons, the old-fashioned pottery and coffeepots, and the smile of the lady handing a plate of pancakes to a hungry sailor."

ENJOY "EATING OUT" AT HOME!

Serve Six for less than $1.00

CHUN KING

CHOW MEIN and CHOP SUEY

Three Choices in BIG New
3 Lb. "Family-Economy" Size...........
...........Now at Your Grocers!

Here is Chow Mein at its rich, savory best. And
so quick to fix. Just heat and serve over crisp Chun King Noodles
or Rice. Six good big servings from the new "family-economy" size.
Your choice of Chicken Chow Mein, Beef Chop Suey, Meatless
Chow Mein. For a wonderful family dinner or when guests
drop in—serve Chun King. Tonight? *Any night!*

© CHUN KING SALES, INC.

Also available in 1 lb. cans to serve 2 or
3 persons . . . look for the Chun King
foods section at your grocers.

1953

thursday was chop suey night

Family who lived in Asia in the '20s brought back a taste for Chinese food.

By Jean Clever, Croton, Ohio

My parents, Anne and Wilford Cossum, were Baptist missionaries in western China from 1920 to 1927. During those years, my sister Caroline and I were born.

After our family's return to Ohio, we often invited our friends and family over for dinner. Mama liked to serve a Chinese banquet on authentic rice-pattern china, while Papa always showed the guests how to use chopsticks.

It was great fun, but Caroline and I, the dishwashers, thought Mama used too many dishes and pans.

Later, during the Depression when money was extremely scarce, the banquet shrank to Mom's chop suey and rice, served with tea, cherries and cake.

Thursday night was chop suey night. It was considered an open house and we could, and did, bring our friends home unannounced. At 25 cents, a pound of hamburger could serve any number as Mama just added more onions and cabbage, which were very inexpensive, celery and a can of bean sprouts, if she could afford them, and sauce.

Our pastor and his wife and sometimes others often came out after choir practice to indulge in a bowl. We thought it was a great treat, as did our friends.

These days we add water chestnuts, bamboo shoots, mushrooms and more celery and bean sprouts to make it special. My friends have marveled that the welcome mat was always out at our home.

SPARE THE HORSES. Jean Clever, below and with brother David and sister Harriet at bottom, explored different modes of transportation while living in China with their missionary parents.

sunday dinners with our grandparents

Weekly rituals were as comforting as the food.

By Becky Schallock, Fountain, Colorado

The resounding smack of the screen door always announced our presence. My father then called out in a booming voice, "Hey, Granny!" That was how every Sunday dinner started when I was a child. These dinners were my favorite, and most memorable, rituals.

Upon entering their open and airy house in Fountain, Colorado, I was transported back in time. The house never changed and, I supposed, never had since my father lived there. Whenever I entered my dad's and aunt's bedrooms, make-up and comic books lay there as though their owners would return at any moment.

My grandparents bustled around the kitchen, cutting meat and filling bowls with steaming vegetables. While Dad relaxed in the worn green leather recliner, my mom, sister and I stood in the kitchen pretending to help while really there just to snitch carrots or olives from the glass relish tray.

When the last dish and cup had been filled, we sat in our chairs. As we all held hands and bowed our heads, Grandpa said grace.

During dinner, the adults talked about work, changes around town or how their animals were doing. My sister and I remained silent. I heard knives and forks clinking against each other. Grandpa began to talk about something, then stammered as he tried to grasp a fleeting thought.

While eating, I could hear the soft clump, not unlike hoofbeats of a horse, coming from Grandpa's false teeth. It was actually a very comforting noise.

Beautiful Bounty

The food on the table was always bountiful and homemade. My favorite part of the dinner was the rolls. They were fresh and served warm.

Grandma made a point of serving them on a dish I bought her for probably 50 cents when I was younger. The plate was ceramic and showed Florida and all the different things the state offered. None of us had ever been there, but I felt proud that she used my gift.

After eating, Grandpa went to the davenport to nap, Dad sat down again in the recliner to read or watch TV, and my sister and I lay on the floor, playing cards.

That left Grandma and Mother to the tedious task of washing dishes. Sometimes I joined them and listened to their conversations about other members of the family or people around town.

I was more of a nuisance than a help. I used to play with the soapy water and would watch the bubbles' prism-like reflections dance in the sunlight. The sound of the plates being stacked signaled that cleanup was done.

We all then gathered around the small kitchen table to play games. As young children, we played Cootie or old maid. As we kids grew older, the games changed to rummy or Tri-Ominos. The sunlight from the kitchen window started to fade behind the mountains, giving the room an orange glow. That was when I knew it was almost time to go.

Sweet So-Long

We'd all get up to say our good-byes. Dad threw his arm around my grandmother to tell her what a great meal it was, and Mom would tell Grandpa that we'd see them again next week.

My sister and I would take our turns saying good-bye. Grandpa would tickle us, then give us each a quick kiss; it was always long enough that his whiskers would scratch our cheeks. Grandma's hug was hard and her kisses soft.

They would walk with us down their rickety, old garage stairs to our car, where Grandma would pretend to push the car out of the driveway. They stood next to each other waving good-bye until we pulled away and the screen door banged shut.

THE GATHERING PLACE.
Grandpa and Grandma Schallock (top) hold hands in their kitchen from the author's story. In the photo above, they pose with Becky Schallock and her sister, Jenny.

monday night stew

When I was growing up in the '50s, Monday was the day Mom baked bread for the rest of the week. Because the oven was in use all day, she always cooked a beef stew on top of the stove for dinner that night.

My sister and I often reminisce about arriving home from school on Monday and eagerly awaiting that delicious stew…big chunks of beef and carrots cooked in thick, tasty, dark brown gravy, served with mashed potatoes and freshly baked bread.

—Marilyn Gordon, Kamloops, British Columbia

OUR FAVORITE GRACE

"When I was in grade school in the early 1940s, we learned this blessing and would say it every day at lunchtime," says Lillye Parket of Fort Wayne, Indiana.

For love, kindness and tender care, for all we eat and all we wear, Father in Heaven, we thank Thee. Amen.

nightly feast

This was a typical dinner scene for my wife's family,
the Pompeis, who lived in Newark, New Jersey. Rachel's
father, Stanley, is seated in the center with his hat on.
I was touched by the fun captured in this 1940 photo.
Their table was always full of food, love and fun.

—*Nick LaSpina, Union, New Jersey*

CHAPTER THREE

Picnics and Parties

Home-cooked dishes always pleased our palates. But, for some reason, the dishes seemed to taste even better at a party…or when dining outdoors.

"In 1937, we kids looked forward to the days when Mom would step on the back porch of our Bartlesville, Oklahoma, home and announce, 'Come get ready. Dad's going to cook Wimpies at the camp,'" says William Wolfenberger of New Market, Tennessee.

"At the campsite, Dad would send us kids to pick up kindling. Once the logs were ready, he would put Mom's heavy cast-iron skillet over the fire. When the pan was nice and hot, he'd add hamburger meat. Then he'd sprinkle a slew of secret ingredients over the sizzling pan. Before long, a wonderful aroma filled the air, even luring other campers to our site.

"Finally, Dad declared, 'Let's eat!' Plates in hand, we'd huddle around the fire, where Dad scooped some his famous Wimpies on buns, topping it with mustard, onions and sweet relish."

The picnic and party tables are full of memories in this chapter, so dig in…

they had a dish to pass for 45 years

By Richard Rundell
Haskell, Oklahoma

Around 1915, two years before I was born, my parents and 11 other couples started taking turns meeting in each other's houses for a potluck supper once a month.

These were truly family get-togethers, as they almost always included the children. All the families lived and farmed around Livingston in southwest Wisconsin, so they called themselves the "Livingston Country Club."

All of the women were excellent cooks. When we hosted the club, my mother made Cornish pasties, a dish handed down from my dad's English ancestors.

In Cornwall, England, miners took pasties to work for their lunches. Pasties are pies with meat and potatoes baked in dough.

Homemade ice cream was also served. The Griswold family had an ice cream freezer that held 2½ gallons. It had a special wheel to crank it that made it easier as the ice cream started to thicken. I also remember Lena Nolan's delicious ice cream because she used all cream instead of part milk and part cream.

The meetings of the club were more than just delicious meals. The women visited and the men played cards. If a meeting was near election time, the men discussed politics.

Polite Politics

But whatever side you were on, no one ever held a grudge over a political belief, or anything else for that matter.

We kids had great fun. In the winter, we played a game we called "Animal Flinch." Each of us took an animal's name, the longer and harder to pronounce, the better.

Then we dealt out specially numbered cards, and each person took turns flipping a card face-up. If the card matched the top card of another, the first to yell out the

LOTS O' POTLUCKERS. Richard Rundell enjoyed the years when the gang got together for potlucks. In this 1944 photo, he's at far left in the back. His sister, Ruby, is standing next to him and their dad, Dale, is sitting in front of him. Mom Laura is seated third from the left.

other's animal name got to give a card to that person. The object was to get rid of all your cards.

In the summer, the club often held Sunday picnics. When my sister, Ruby, and I were in our teens, we helped the club get together by phoning all the members. We called it "getting up a picnic."

The picnics were usually held near a creek, or "crick" as we called it. I learned to swim in a creek during those picnics. Others would go fishing, like the time Azel Griswold, then 8 and the youngest of the Country Club children, walked back from where he had been fishing.

"I thought you were fishing," someone said. "Where are your fish?"

"Here," Azel said with a big smile, and he pulled a fish out of his pocket.

In addition to the regular Country Club potluck suppers, three of the families often got together for Sunday dinner—Ted Griswold's, Uncle Henry's and ours.

I remember one winter Sunday when we had been snowed in for several days because the county plow hadn't been down our road. Delphia Griswold called and invited us for dinner.

We hitched the team to the bobsled, and with Ruby, Mother and me huddled down with blankets, Dad drove the sled over the snow-covered roads and fields five miles to the Griswolds' place.

The club demonstrated solid family values. Our farm parents struggled through the Depression and worked hard to keep their farms, so we were taught early in life about work and responsibility.

Memories of the Livingston Country Club are a joy to me.

cool treat

The highlight at our family reunions was the ice cream served in the afternoon to refresh everyone. This photo was taken in June 1941 at the first reunion of the William Meissner family. Darwin Meissner is serving the ice cream as his kin eagerly await their turns. I'm the tall girl in the center.
—*Marjorie Schlei*
Sussex, Wisconsin

M·M·M·M. . . . "kitchen-fresh" Frankfurters

MADE OF FINE ARMOUR BEEF AND PORK

Hot Supper—in a Hurry!

A double-quick dinner—that's doubly good! Armour Star Frankfurters with Armour Star Chili Con Carne! And what a fine fresh flavor these frankfurters have . . . because they're plump with *Armour* beef and pork! Flavorful, tender pork and beef at their fresh-tasting best! For Armour Star Frankfurters are made "Kitchen-Fresh" daily in scores of Armour Kitchens all across the country and rushed from the nearest one to your market. Have them this way soon:

Chili Red Hots

Heat 1 lb. of Armour Star Frankfurters this way: Have a pan of boiling water, add frankfurters, remove pan from heat, cover tightly and leave for 7 or 8 min. Heat 1 can Armour Star Chili Con Carne to boiling. Arrange frankfurters in a deep platter, pour the Chili Con Carne over them. Serve with slices of French bread that have been buttered, topped with dill pickle slices and heated in 400° F. oven for 10 min. or until lightly browned.

For other new and interesting sausage recipes, write
Marie Gifford, Dept. 62, P. O. Box 2053, Chicago 9, Ill.

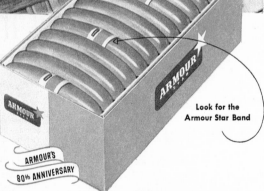

Look for the
Armour Star Band

ARMOUR'S
80th ANNIVERSARY

The best and nothing but the best is labeled ARMOUR★

1947

picnics were part of the landscape

Fun Brightened Days of the Depression

In the '30s, the American Legion picnic was a red-letter day for us kids in the small rural town of Enterprise, Oregon.

Long tables were covered with an assortment of tablecloths and piled high with food prepared by our moms. Each mother brought the dish she was "famous" for, so we were treated to the town's best cooking. My mom, Olive Heasty, always fixed her specialty, a crock of slow-baked beans.

We kids had all the soda pop we could drink and all the ice cream we could eat. The soda pop was kept cold in washtubs filled with ice. All we had to do was grab a bottle and run.

The vanilla ice cream was brought from the creamery in heavy metal cylinders packed in rock salt and ice. We could have a cone every time we turned around. It was magic.

There was lots of laughter and singing of World War I songs like *Hinky Dinky Parlay Voo*. I've never known a more patriotic group than Daddy and his WWI buddies. I was very proud of them.

We kids played ball and other games while our parents visited. When the sun went down behind the Wallowa Mountains, we packed up the remains of the day and went home to bed and sweet dreams.

All of this took place during the Depression, and there was poverty all around us. But somehow the American Legion picnic made up for what we didn't have or couldn't get.

On that wonderful day, we thought we were the luckiest kids in the world.

—*Claudine Willis, Portland, Oregon*

PLENTY OF FOOD FOR ALL. "This photo was taken in the mid-1930s, during the Depression," says Edward Rappold, Cedarburg, Wisconsin. "Food stamps were scarce, but my parents had three acres of land to grow fruits and vegetables. During the summer, they often invited relatives and friends out to the country for a Sunday picnic."

A PICNIC FOR THE PATRIARCH.

The McGee clan convened on July 12, 1944, to celebrate the 100th anniversary of the birth of Joseph McGee, who was the family patriarch. Joseph, who had died in 1911, was the grandfather of Harold McGee, from Byron, Georgia, who shared the above photo.

"Joseph's oldest son, Perry (my father), got the old home place when Joseph divided the property," Harold explains. "That's where this gathering was held."

No paper plates in those days. Looks like plenty of good eats, though, with kettles simmering in the background, and glasses of iced tea to wash it all down, as the relatives wait patiently for this photo to be taken.

Happiness is like potato salad—the minute you share it, it becomes a picnic.

AS THEY WERE. "In this group photo of the 'Go As You Are Club,' I'm the girl in the front row, second from the right," says Esmond Davis Taylor. "My mother, Gladys Davis, would have been in the photo in the space in the back row, but she snapped the picture."

ladies club was friendly and casual
Food, fun and fellowship were the agenda.

By Esmond Davis Taylor, Coshocton, Ohio

In the '40s, a number of ladies living in rural Coshocton County, Ohio, formed a club. My mother told me they wanted it to be friendly and down-to-earth, so they called it the "Go As You Are" club.

Every month, the ladies met at the home of one of the members. They each brought a dish to pass. Before lunch there was a short meeting with devotionals, and after lunch there was some type of entertainment.

In the summer, we daughters got to tag along. We were sometimes asked to participate in the entertainment by singing, dancing, playing an instrument or even putting on a short play.

But for us, the best part of the meeting was the lunch. Our mothers tried to outdo each other by fixing their best dishes, and there was always enough for seconds.

MINI UNITED NATIONS. I grew up in a small but diverse ethnic neighborhood in Peckville, Pennsylvania, near Scranton. The women were a very close-knit group that frequently met for coffee and often shared their favorite ethnic recipes.

My mom, Ada Paoletti, was born in Italy, Bertha Puletti was Polish, Alice Sebastianelli was Lithuanian and Grace Lemoncelli was Italian. Mom taught Bertha and Alice how to make spaghetti sauce, and they taught my mom and Grace how to make pierogis and other Polish foods.

This photo (right) shows the group in 1949 at one of its coffee klatches. From left to right are Grace, Bertha, Alice and my mom.

—*Jean Meka, Vestal, New York*

remember 'come as you are' parties?

By Katie Adams, Red Oak, Texas

A favorite memory from the '50s was watching my mom get "pegged" for a "Come as You Are" party.

It always happened in the morning with a knock at the door, and when Mom opened it, the hostess who "pegged" her took exact notes on how she was dressed—nightgown, curlers and all!

Whoever hosted the party that morning would go around and "peg" the others to later meet at her house. The hostess usually served coffee and coffee cake or pastries.

The party started later, after the kids were at school, and everyone had to show up exactly as "pegged." If you were wearing a towel, you arrived in a towel!

We lived in a suburb of Louisville, Kentucky, and Mom was on the Ladies' Auxiliary for the volunteer fire department. (These ladies would have a meal ready for the firemen whenever they got back from a call.) This same group of

GOTCHA! A 1957 "Come as You Are" party caught Katie Adams' mother, Helen Fisher (third from left), in a robe and with a roller in her bangs.

about 10 ladies started having a "Come as You Are" party once a month.

Mom was always fussy about looking her best and curled her bangs every morning. One thing she hated was getting pegged with her roller in!

After one party, Mom stewed for two days about "getting pegged with that roller in." Daddy loved it! Mom and Dad still live in the same house where the five of us kids grew up, and we all laugh about those times.

Many mothers work today, so few would be able to make the time for such simple pleasures.

OUR FAVORITE GRACE

"My grandchildren like me to say this grace when they visit because I tell them my grandpa said it when I was a little girl," shares Ruthie Bamburg of West Monroe, Louisiana.

Merciful Father, smile upon us.
Make us truly thankful for these
and all Thy many blessings.
In Jesus' name, Amen.

taffy pull parties were sweet

By Evelyn Agenbroad, Emmett, Idaho

Clothesline taffy! As I was growing up in the '30s, just mentioning the name to our family of seven kids filled the air with excitement.

Not only was taffy a treat, but it meant we'd have company at our ranch in New Mexico. It took many buttered hands to bring this sticky specialty to perfection. And in the days before television, this was our entertainment.

We didn't have electricity back in the 1930s, so all cooking was done on our Majestic wood range. December through February was a good time for taffy since keeping the stove hot for the candy helped heat the house. And we needed the cold weather outside to cure it.

In those days, we started with sugar, corn syrup, gelatin, paraffin and milk. We cooked the taffy until it was brittle in cold water, then poured it into a well-buttered sheet pan and set it out to cool.

Every few minutes, we'd knead it and try to work it into a ball. It was still very hot and took several tries to get it cool enough to be handled. Then, with well-buttered hands, the first pullers worked the candy together until they could form it into a rope and begin stretching it, a little at a time. It was important to run their hands the full length of the rope each time to work all of it and keep it intact.

Many Hands Make Short Work

Their hands got very warm, and we made sure more pullers were standing by with buttered hands to take over. As the taffy cooled, little strands would leave the main rope—and the children were there, eager to catch the first piece.

As the taffy was pulled, it got harder and the rope got very long. Sometimes you had to back up to be able to keep your feet anchored—especially if the person on the other end was heftier.

Friends and family pulled together as the ropes of candy cooled and stiffened.

The candy was light brown when we started and got lighter as it stretched. It was easy to get anxious and not keep on pulling. When it was ready, it had separated into several ropes, and running our hands over it wouldn't keep it together.

When it was as light as possible, we placed the strands on a clean sheet, then folded the sheet over the clothesline to harden, hence the name "clothesline taffy."

When it was completely cold, we could bring it in. It was so brittle that placing the sheet on a hard surface would break the taffy into pieces. What was left after we all sampled our fill was placed in airtight containers and was shared with friends and neighbors.

After my husband, Stanley, and I were married and had children, we loved having neighbors and family members come and join in the fellowship, pulling taffy—and making lots of great memories.

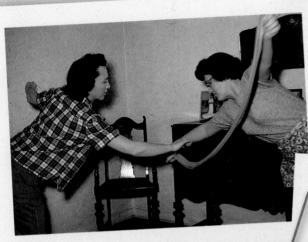

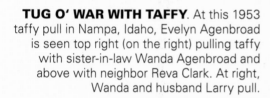

TUG O' WAR WITH TAFFY. At this 1953 taffy pull in Nampa, Idaho, Evelyn Agenbroad is seen top right (on the right) pulling taffy with sister-in-law Wanda Agenbroad and above with neighbor Reva Clark. At right, Wanda and husband Larry pull.

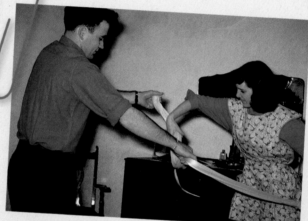

OUR FAVORITE GRACE

"I care for three little children frequently," says *Valerie Larkin from Stonewall, Manitoba. "Watching them with their eyes tightly closed and their tiny hands folded when we say this grace truly warms my heart."*

Thank you, God, for food so good, and help us do the things we should. Amen.

light

right

ready

Reddi wip WHIPPED CREAM

it's real whipped cream

Today's busy mother knows ... Reddi-Wip is

the easy, modern way to serve real whipped cream.

It's light, low in calories, flavored right

and always ready ... delightfully nutritious

too ... because it's real whipped cream.

ALSO AVAILABLE IN CANADA

© 1958 R. W. INC.

1958

birthdays were something to celebrate

Birthdays are nature's way of telling us to eat more cake.

PLEASE PASS THE CAKE. I am the lad on the right at this celebration in honor of my fifth birthday, in 1945. My mother made the day quite memorable by seating us around the dining room table. I still have that treasured table, which inspires many happy memories.

—*Donald Mackey, Crestwood, Missouri*

HAVE YOUR CAKE AND EAT IT, TOO! Grace Scowen of Kelowna, British Columbia, bakes a special cake for the birthdays of her children, grandchildren and great-grandchildren. In this 1947 photo, son Bruce (center, with sailor collar) is the guest of honor.

birthday party on a shoestring was still sensational

This young couple celebrated postwar apartment with a party for their firstborn.

By Dolores Eggener, Marinette, Wisconsin

We moved into our first apartment in 1946, but it was another year or so until our lives finally settled down.

We slowly transformed the apartment in Marinette, Wisconsin, into a home as furniture became available in stores. In those early postwar years, you couldn't just walk in and buy a living room or bedroom suite—your name went on a list.

HOT DOG, IT'S MY BIRTHDAY! Birthday boy Jimmy Eggener was 2 in 1947, when his mom and dad gave him a party with a circus theme that included hot dogs in homemade barbecue sauce and a from-scratch cake topped with animal crackers. Dolores Eggener's brother, Jack Kmiecik, took these photos above.

When it was our turn, we got a call telling us what was available. We bought our living room furniture sight unseen.

"It's blue," they told us. "Fine!" we said.

Refrigerators were especially hard to come by, but we were fortunate to have been moved up on the list because we had a baby, our son, Jimmy.

The problem was, when the refrigerator became available, the money wasn't. We decided to sell my husband Dick's large stamp collection to finance the purchase. We had our priorities!

Finally outfitted with all the necessary appliances and furniture, we decided to celebrate by having a birthday party for Jimmy, who turned 2 in April 1947.

I decided on a circus theme. Jimmy was all in favor, and it fit our budget. Two candles and animal crackers pulling tinted marshmallow carts adorned the homemade layer cake, the first of hundreds I would make in my life.

Pear halves became clown faces with clove eyes and noses, cherry mouths and cream cheese details. There were Jell-O cubes for color, and a cupcake topped with an animal cracker marked each place. The main course was hot dogs baked in my homemade barbecue sauce, along with potato salad. Guests were grandparents, uncles, an aunt and one cousin.

We've had a parade of birthdays for our eventual brood of six, and I've managed to come up with many unique ideas for their parties. Each celebration was special, and this one from so long ago was a great beginning.

WELCOME HOME! My daddy's homemade three-flavored, multitiered cake in 1960 was not only his birthday cake, but welcomed him home after a year's work in New Jersey, away from the family in Benton County, Tennessee. Since his birthday was December 23, the table and room were decorated with homemade Christmas decorations that my mom had made.

—*Ginger Dicerson Canfield*
Madison, Alabama

BIRTHDAY "BOY." When I was a child growing up in Nowata, Oklahoma, my Pop was full of high jinks. In this 1958 photo celebrating in 65th birthday, you can almost see the mischief in his smile. No doubt he's clowning it up, much to the delight of his grandson Dale. Pop was a great man, who taught me to be honest, dependable and everything else we want children to be.

—*Jayne Kennedy Sweger*
Great Falls, Montana

tea for ten

Little girl felt grown-up on her eighth birthday.

By Suzanne Jones, Granbury, Texas

This tea party was for my future sister-in-law, Darlene Jones Crouch (second from left in the photo above), who now lives in Newport News, Virginia. It was her eighth birthday, May 4, 1948.

Her little friends were asked to wear dress-up clothes and bring their dolls. At the party, each girl was given a wrist corsage made from a paper doily, ribbons and paper flowers.

The cake was angel food. There was a maypole in the center of the eight candles, with ribbons leading to the party favors. It was all lovingly prepared by Darlene's mother, and now my mother-in-law, Maudetha Jones. Darlene recalls it as the best birthday party ever!

The girls were delighted with being served from the silver tea service seen on the counter at left and using the demitasse cups of "fine china."

I am now the proud owner of the tea service, and my daughter, Lacey Henson, received the china as a very special wedding gift from her grandmother.

put out the fire

When Ann Janis of Tucson, Arizona, blew out the candles on her 50th birthday cake, in '61, her husband, Stan, her mom and neighbor kids Craig and Lisa joined the fun. Craig also gave Ann a helping breath so he could get at some of that cake faster.

CHAPTER FOUR

Kitchen Capers

Whether you're experienced in the kitchen or still a little wet behind the ears, our attempts to cook and bake are sometimes a recipe for disaster.

"When my husband and I were dating, he lived with his aunt and uncle, who had a beautiful cherry tree in their yard. They were going away for a week and invited me to pick the cherries while they were gone," says Pat Hauck, Hummelstown, Pennsylvania.

"I decided to surprise my boyfriend with a homemade pie. I got a ladder, picked the cherries and washed them, made my own crust, prepared the filling and baked the pie.

"Oh, that pie smelled good. Then I thought I'd better taste it before giving it to him. Well, the first bite felt like my mouth was full of small marbles! You guessed it…I forgot to take out the pits! I threw the pie away and cried."

Sure, mistakes in the kitchen can sometimes be the pits, but what lasting, light-hearted memories they make.

mama's little chicken fixer

*By Betty Black Holder Autry
Lillington, North Carolina (as told to
Beatrice Black Bullard Barfield)*

The year was 1919. I was 7 years old, and Mama was sick in bed with a migraine headache at our home outside Lillington, North Carolina.

Since Daddy couldn't miss work, I was to take care of my three younger brothers for the day. (Our baby sister was 3 months old and could stay in bed with Mama.)

Before he left, Daddy killed a chicken and carefully explained how to scald it and pick off the feathers. He told me to cook it and put rice in the stock for us to eat. "Maybe it will make your mother feel better," he added.

The cookstove was still hot from breakfast, and there was hot water in the kettle. I knew it needed to be boiling, so I added some more wood and soon the kettle lid was jiggling with steam.

Daddy had made a little footstool for me to stand on to help Mama wash dishes. I dragged it over to the stove so I could reach the kettle. I managed to get it off the stove without getting burned and carried it to the back porch, where the chicken waited in an old tin washtub.

After pouring boiling water over the chicken, I picked it up by the feet and swirled it around in the water like I'd seen Mama do. The feathers came off easily.

Next I carried the chicken to the fireplace in the kitchen to singe it. After putting some paper on the hot coals, I quickly turned the bird over in the flames. (The odor reminded me of the time Daddy accidentally scorched his coat in the fireplace.)

There were ashes on the chicken afterward, so I decided I'd better wash it and took the chicken out to the back porch.

Filling the water bucket with our gourd dipper, I grabbed a bar of Mama's homemade lye soap and started scrubbing our dinner clean!

Mama wanted me to bring the chicken

GROWN-UP COOK. By the time this photo of Betty Autry and her son was taken in the 1940s, she had mastered the job of cooking—no more cleaning chickens with lye soap!

to her when I finished, so I carried it into the bedroom. "How did you get it so clean?" she asked.

When I told her I'd washed it with soap and water, she explained that I'd have to rinse it with clear water at least four times.

Back to the porch I went! But now the pump had lost its prime, so I had to go to the well for water to prime it. After I finally got the chicken rinsed, I had another problem—it had to be cut up.

I wasn't afraid of the butcher knife, since Granddaddy had taught me how to use it. But after cutting off the wings and legs, I had trouble getting the chicken apart—I just wasn't strong enough.

Back in the bedroom, I asked Mama what to do. She instructed my 5-year-old brother to help and, between the two of us, we got the job done. After I finished cleaning and cutting, I finally got the chicken into the pot.

Although Daddy hadn't told me to make bread, I'd seen Mama fix biscuits and wanted to try. Mixing flour, lard and buttermilk, I made dough and put it in a pan—it looked like one large biscuit!

Mama told me that when I could stick a fork into the chicken easily to add about a cup and a half of rice to the pot. I took samples of the rice to her in a saucer until she was certain it was done.

That chicken and rice and my giant "biscuit" satisfied our hunger, and there was enough left over for supper later on. It must have helped Mama, too, because I remember seeing her asleep that afternoon.

Seventy-eight years later, I can still remember the warm glow I felt when Daddy praised me that night, calling me a "little woman." While I certainly played the part of a woman that day, I shudder now to think of all the things that could have gone wrong the time I fixed a chicken for Mama.

OUR FAVORITE GRACE

"I remember I had to be very quiet when my grandfather said this blessing," says *Bettie Thomas of Lakeland, Florida.*

Kind Heavenly Father, smile down upon us, pardon all our wrongs, make us thankful for this food prepared for our bodies. We ask this in Jesus' name and for His sake. Amen.

WHEN IT RAINS

Plain or iodized

IT POURS

More people use Morton's

1951

kids in the kitchen

Their first attempts at cooking often left youngsters with a bad taste in their mouths.

The Recipe Seemed So Simple...

When I was in high school, I saw a colorful ad for a beautiful gelatin dessert and decided to make it after supper.

The instructions appeared easy—you made three colors of Jell-O and layered them in parfait glasses. Every other layer was whipped, and the layers were slanted.

Since we didn't have parfait glasses, I rounded up 12 drinking glasses. The first clear layer went into the glasses and was ready for the refrigerator. Now a new problem—making room for all those glasses and tilting them without falling over.

Next, in order for the Jell-O to whip, it had to be cooled to the thickness of egg whites. This took time, and I suddenly realized that I should have started this project in the morning, on a day I didn't have to go to school.

After a couple of layers, the Jell-O started getting too firm to whip, even at room temperature. And now the other colors that were to be poured clear were too thick to pour.

Mother had gone to bed, so I was on my own. The kitchen was a mess, filled with bowls of clear and whipped Jell-O, and it was already way past my bedtime. By the time I finished, it was past midnight! I don't remember what the final results looked like— not picture-book pretty, I'm sure.

Of course, it was all edible, but since there were only Mom, Dad and me to eat it, those desserts probably lasted several days. That was one recipe I never repeated.

—*Caroline Hix Burke, Yukon, Oklahoma*

A Vesuvian Overflow

When I was a child, we were on welfare and regularly received large sacks of Gold Medal flour. Making bread was a routine at our house, and all the children had their turn.

Eventually it was my turn. The dough was always mixed the night before so it would be ready to bake in the morning. Pop placed the tub in the center of the kitchen table and I went to work, measuring and mixing the ingredients.

When it came time to add the yeast, I yelled to my mother in the living room, "How much yeast, Mom?" And she yelled back, "One."

In the morning, when Mom came into the kitchen to start breakfast, she could hardly get into the room...white, gooey globs were all over the table, chairs and floor, like white lava flowing down from Mt. Vesuvius.

In response to her "one," I threw in one whole box of yeast, when she meant just one of the small pie-shaped pieces.

—*Donald Ulrich, Chula Vista, California*

Fudge Foiled Their Fun

One summer day in the early 1940s, my sister and I were left home while our parents were away on a trip. We two teenage girls had a hankering for fudge and got to work in the kitchen.

We mixed, cooked, stirred...and burned the fudge to the bottom of one of Mother's favorite pans. Try as we may, the hardened mess wouldn't come off. What were we to do? Why, hide the evidence, of course!

There was a huge lilac tree in our backyard, the base of which was surrounded by dozens of leafy sprigs and vines. It was the perfect place to hide the pot of fudge. Deep into the greenery it went, never to be seen until the tree was cut down years later.

—Nancy Neimeyer
Fogelsville, Pennsylvania

Frosting Took the Cake

While my parents were at a farm auction one day in the '40s, I tried baking my first cake. I was quite successful, but the frosting, however, proved to be a challenge.

I chose a boiled frosting...followed the directions, cooking it until it formed a bubble when dropped in water. To be on the safe side, I boiled it a little longer. Though I managed to cover the cake, it became a difficult procedure. By the time I was almost done, the spatula was stuck, rock-hard, in the pan.

When my parents came home, I made coffee and we attempted to have cake, but we couldn't get the knife through the frosting! We finally removed the frosting in one piece, broke it up and ate it as though it was peanut brittle.

—Robert Hammerschmidt
Mosinee, Wisconsin

OUR FAVORITE GRACE

"One year at a Junior Boys' Church Camp, one 9-year-old camper offered this prayer before the evening meal. He was most earnest and sincere," *says Sheila Free of Red Deer, Alberta.*

Dear Lord, help us to like the food we are about to eat.

pressure cooker catastrophes

Cooks were steamed when failure to release pressure resulted in a mess.

Ham to High Heaven

To welcome me home for a visit in the 1960s, my mom cooked a ham in the pressure cooker. One thing I wanted to do was attend an auction at a nearby farm. So Mom turned off the stove and we headed out.

After we got home, Mom turned the stove on again to continue cooking dinner. Within moments, there was a loud explosion from the pressure that had built up in the cooker.

Bits of ham were all over Mom's newly wallpapered kitchen walls. Mom never made that mistake again…and I vowed never to use a pressure cooker in my home!

—*Florence Stovall, Coeur d'Alene, Idaho*

First Thanksgiving Was Memorable

I'd been in the United States for a very short time in 1954, so my supervisor invited me over for Thanksgiving dinner. I was so impressed with the warmth and comfort of her home and the table, set with her best china and silver.

I offered to help and was assigned the task of making the mashed potatoes. I was to watch a huge pot with a heavy lid, a pressure cooker, for about 10 minutes. When the small weight on top started to rattle, I was told the desired pressure had been reached inside and the potatoes were done. I had never seen such a contraption and didn't have the faintest idea how to turn it off to stop the cooking. So I took the pot off the burner and slowly opened the lid. Out came the potatoes in full force, hitting the ceiling first, then the walls, kitchen curtains and counters. Potatoes were everywhere.

Well, Thanksgiving dinner started a little late, but I still had a wonderful day, a great meal and more than my share to be thankful for.

—*Marieluise Harrar, Tucson, Arizona*

Sauerkraut Explosion

The first time I used my pressure cooker, I read the directions carefully and thought I understood how it worked. I brought the pressure up to 15 pounds but forgot to release the pressure cap. Thinking there couldn't be that much pressure under the lid, I took it off.

Well, the thing just blew. When my husband came home from work, he found me on the ladder, scraping clumps of sauerkraut off the ceiling. We ate what remained in the pot, and the pork was so tender, it fell off the bone. It was delicious.

—Mary Cooper, San Bernardino, California

Meal Was a Misadventure

Mom's kitchen was her palace—it was fastidiously maintained and everything was always in its place. The room was beautifully decorated in lavender and muted pink. There was a kitchen table with matching chairs, and African violets adorned the windowsill over the sink. It was where Mom took pride in serving her family meticulously planned meals each night.

One evening in the late '40s or early '50s, Mom was preparing zucchini in her trusty pressure cooker. Pressure cookers were a great invention for home cooks. Food was placed on a metal rack in the pot of a heavy aluminum pot and water was added to just below the rim of the metal rack. You would twist the lid with its rubber seal onto the pot and set the gauge on top for how long you wanted to steam the food. The little gauge would flutter and jump as the desired temperature inside the pressure cooker was reached.

For some reason that night, Mom forgot a crucial step in the process—releasing the pressure inside before twisting open the lid. Instead, Mom removed the pressure cooker from the stove and immediately proceeded to open it up. Dinner was served…on the ceiling.

Mom was beside herself. Mushy bits of zucchini were all over her clean kitchen. Dad climbed on a stool and salvaged what he could.

To make matters worse, when Mom pulled the tray of Swedish meatballs from the oven onto the oven door, the door didn't hold the weight. Saucy meatballs splashed across the floor and were chased by our Persian cat.

Eventually, all we could do was laugh…even Mom. Yes, our family survived the only disastrous dinner I can remember.

—Richard Gartrell, Warrenton, Oregon

If at first you don't succeed, you have two choices—try again or read the instructions.

Those never-fail cooks

...the MILK TEST spills their secret!

Those happy, happy folks who *never* miss with the rave-getting dishes—how *do* they do it? By making sure things cook *evenly*. That's *so* easy— with Wear-Ever! Food-friendly Wear-Ever aluminum utensils spread heat so fast, so evenly, you can actually do this: Pour a pint of milk into a Wear-Ever Sauce Pan, put it directly over low heat. Now—you can boil it down to ¼ pint *without stirring* and *without scorching!* *Every* Wear-Ever utensil has this fast-, even-heating quality—a vital aid to *never*-miss cooking!

Taste-tempting dishes come from Wear-Ever Covered Sauce Pots! Easy-to-clean Steam-Seal cover, cool Bakelite knob. Cup-marked for easy measuring.

Made of the metal that cooks best . . . easy to clean

WEAR·EVER
Aluminum
UTENSILS

THE ALUMINUM COOKING UTENSIL CO.,
NEW KENSINGTON, PA.

Wear-Ever Pressure Cooker! Reaches temperature fast, then cooks cabbage, say, in 2 minutes! Vegetables stay garden-fresh, meats richly juicy. Patented Snap-Tite Cover can't come off while pressure is on.

©1947 T.A.C.U.CO.

Wear-Ever 3-Way Combination gives you three utensils in one—a covered sauce pan, a double boiler *and* a baking dish or casserole! Smart new modern styling!

1947

men at the range made mistakes, too

When dads offered to help in the kitchen, bloopers weren't far behind.

Pop's Cooking Blunder Was a Happy Accident

Mom usually did the cooking for the family in our Stratford, New Jersey, home, but one day she decided to visit her sister overnight. She left Friday after dinner, assured by Pop that he could handle making breakfast for seven kids and himself.

The next morning, we showed up in the kitchen, hungry as usual. Pop got toast started in the woodstove's big oven, then added oatmeal to the boiling water. He got extremely busy, as the oatmeal had to be stirred to keep it from sticking and the toast had to be turned to keep it from burning.

He almost lost it when the pot of milk for the hot cocoa showed signs of coming to a boil. He reached for the cocoa can, lifted the lid on the oatmeal pot and shoveled several scoops of powdered cocoa into the near-ready oatmeal.

When he saw his error, Pop quickly added Hershey's cocoa to the milk, but the oatmeal was another matter. There was no time to redo the whole breakfast and keep seven hungry kids from revolting.

So while one of the older kids poured the hot cocoa, Pop ladled out heaping dishes of his newly invented chocolate oatmeal, selling the merits as he dished. We really believed he cooked up this new breakfast treat especially for us. We added sugar and milk and ate it all.

The incident wasn't mentioned until the next Saturday morning, when Mom tried to serve some of the anemic regular oatmeal. Even though it was decorated with sugar, butter and fresh milk, it paled in comparison to Pop's chocolate oatmeal.   —Lou Rodia
Cape May Court House, New Jersey

Special Delivery

Back when my three children were young, our niece and nephew also lived with us. While my wife was at work one day, I decided to bake a white cake complete with pink icing.

Because the kitchen was hot from baking the cake, I decided to put the cake in the garage to cool, setting it safely out of the way on the roof of my station wagon.

A while later, my niece called and said she needed a ride home from town, which is a seven-mile round-trip. So I jumped in the car and off I drove. When we returned, I put the car in the garage and shut the garage door.

It wasn't until after dinner when everyone asked "What's for dessert?" that I remembered the cake.

"Oh, no!" I cried as I jumped up and ran to the garage. There sat the pink cake up against the luggage rack on the roof of the car. It leaned a little, but it had sure cooled off during its seven-mile ride. We ate every last slice.

—*Paul LaBar, Bangor, Pennsylvania*

Tapioca Was a Fiasco

While Mother was in the hospital with the new baby, Dad had to cook. He only knew how to make pancakes and fried eggs, but he thought he would expand his repertoire and asked what we would like. We kids agreed—our favorite dish was Mother's tapioca pudding.

Not knowing he had to presoak the pearl tapioca, Dad simply put it on to boil…much too hard. He put it in the oven to bake…still not edible. Finally, he sliced and fried it. No longer did it resemble tapioca pudding. We tried to eat the hard, rubbery, dark stuff but gave up.

—*Warren Olin*
Owego, New York

love blinds the taste buds

Newlyweds lived on love...not her cooking.

By Anne Ferguson, Conyers, Georgia

When Carl and I married in 1962, I was so in love that I figured everything in marriage would come naturally.

Surprise! I could not cook, no matter how hard I tried.

I don't know how Carl survived, although Alka-Seltzer always followed each meal like it was dessert.

One evening, I decided to cook a special dinner. Carl came home to a wonderful aroma, a beautifully set table and soft music. The menu was steak, creamed potatoes, salad, rolls and pie for dessert.

Carl and I began to saw the steak and chewed and chewed. We actually cut bites out of the creamed potatoes because I had whipped them for at least 30 minutes.

As Carl was preparing his Alka-Seltzer, he asked where I had purchased the roast and why I had broiled it instead of boiling or baking it.

Surprised, I yelled that it was not a roast.

He hugged me gently and said not to worry; he loved our dinner together.

I was so embarrassed. I didn't even know a steak from a roast or which way to cook either one. My pride kept me from consulting either of our mothers.

Thank goodness for my father-in-law, who was sensitive enough to give me a Betty Crocker cookbook. He placed it on the counter without saying a word.

I started asking more questions, and it turned out Carl knew more about cooking than I did.

After about two years, Carl no longer chased each meal with Alka-Seltzer.

EAT YOUR HEART OUT.
Love overcame Anne Ferguson's inability to cook for her husband, Carl.

"A" for Effort

The first time I invited my in-laws over for supper, I chose to make a roast and called my mom for instructions. She told me to add water but didn't say how much, so I covered the roast with water. It came out like boiled soup meat, only with no flavor.

As a thoughtful gesture, I also baked my in-laws a custard pie to take home. I had forgotten to scald the milk, though, and the texture was like scrambled eggs.

I'm sure they felt sorry for their son, whose wife didn't know the first thing about cooking.

—*Frances Dohr, Affton, Missouri*

Not Like Mom Used to Make

Shortly after I was married in 1964, I decided to surprise my husband with his favorite cookie. I called Madge, my mother-in-law, who wrote down her chocolate chip cookie recipe for a double batch. While assembling the ingredients, I dashed to the store for more chocolate chips.

After removing the first tray of cookies from the oven, they just poured off the cookie sheet. I called my mother-in-law and discovered she forgot to write a dash between 2 – 6 ounces of chips. Yes, I added 26 ounces of chocolate chips!

I tried to salvage the batter, but it all ended up in the trash. We all still laugh about this blunder.

—*Marquetta Fouts, Stafford, Virginia*

They Ate Like Birds

As a young newlywed, I was serving guests for the first time in our home. I was so proud of my beautifully mixed salad.

I couldn't resist one final touch, so I reached into my handy spice rack and lavishly sprinkled the contents from one of the prettiest containers. Imagine my surprise when, returning the container to the rack, I discovered I had added Budgie Parakeet Treat!

What to do? I had to have a salad! I hurriedly checked the ingredients, found nothing harmful, crossed my fingers and served it to my guests. Surprisingly, I received many compliments and no one knew the secret…until now!

—*Genevieve Kasten, Mt. Clemens, Michigan*

The trouble with getting it right the first time is no one appreciates how difficult it was.

where there's smoke...

Smoke signals were telltale sign that it was time eat.

Don't Be Alarmed

I thought everything had to be cooked at a high temperature when I first got married. Consequently, the smoke alarm frequently went off when I was making dinner. My husband had gotten so used to the sound that he hardly noticed it anymore.

One night, the alarm once again went off, and our downstairs neighbor charged up the stairs and burst into our apartment. He found my husband sitting on the couch, watching TV.

"I thought your apartment was on fire!" he exclaimed. To which my husband calmly replied, "No, it's just Kendra cooking dinner."
—*Kendra Antila*
Lebanon, Oregon

Toasters Were Tricky

When my husband, Jim, and I were first married in 1953 and living in Flint, Michigan, we had a toaster that you had to flip the toast from one side to the other.

I was making bacon and eggs one morning and asked him to watch the toast for me. Pretty soon, he started calling my name over and over.

"What do you want?" I asked with some irritation.

"The toast is burning," he said.

He noted that all I'd asked him to do was watch the toast.

Many few years later, we purchased a travel trailer. It never seems to fail that when I make toast inside the trailer, the smoke alarm goes off.

One morning when that happened, we heard a fellow camper say, "Breakfast is ready!" Now Jim likes to tell everyone that when the smoke detector goes off, he knows dinner is served.
—*Marilyn Henderson*
Alpena, Michigan

ingredient spoiled the broth

Mother often made stews, soups or chili in the deep well cooker on her electric stove. One time, after she had stirred the soup, she replaced the lid but didn't see the hot pad stuck to the lid. At dinner, when she began to ladle out the soup, she felt something strange and bulky at the bottom, which she retrieved with a cooking fork. Up came the dripping, steaming hot pad. There had to be a quick alternative for supper that night, and the dogs got the soup…maybe even the hot pad!

—*Theodora Link, Columbia Heights, Minnesota*

CHAPTER FIVE

Dining Out Adventures

As much as we enjoyed savoring one of Mom's home-cooked meals, there was something special about sitting down to a table at a restaurant, soda fountain or diner…even when the foods were no different than home.

"In 1944, when I was 9 years old and living in Los Angeles, I delivered the local paper twice a week," says Bob Denzil Lee of Nuevo, California. "When I finished my route, I often stopped at a small diner for a waffle and a glass of milk.

"Mom usually made waffles for us on weekends, so Dad could not understand why I spent my money on something I could eat at home.

"Here's why: The family waffle iron was one of those that made four rectangular waffle sections. That meant after sharing half with my brother, I had to wait through several rounds before I got the rest of my breakfast!

"At the diner, I not only got my full waffle, but it was round, which automatically made it taste better. All that pleasure for 20 cents a week was worth it."

Yes, eating out was a guaranteed good time.

nothing was finer than

the Auburn Diner

By Deanna Provines
Auburn, Indiana

When my mother, Jessie Rohm, bought the Auburn Diner in Auburn, Indiana, I got a raise from 35 cents to 50 cents an hour. I started working as a waitress at the diner in 1953, when I was 13. I worked for Herman Tritch, the son-in-law of the man who started the diner, "Dad" Shuman. My mother bought the diner the next year.

The diner was actually an old streetcar that was brought in and set on a basement foundation. All the cooking was done in the basement. The diner had one long counter with 10 stools and two short counters with three stools each. And all of those stools were usually full of customers, many of whom were regulars.

Regular Cast of Characters

The courthouse was across the street, and we got a lot of customers from there. One woman who worked at the courthouse was diabetic, so my mother always cooked something special for her. In fact, although there was a menu every day, Mom would cook something special for anyone who asked…like the three ladies from the courthouse who every once in a while would say, "Well, Jet, we're going on a diet."

Mom was known as "Jet" because she was always on a dead run in the diner.

Another regular was Judge Harold Stump, who came in for lunch every day. On Monday, when the menu was ham and beans, he'd say, "I'll have a ham and a bean." Then he'd bury his nose in the newspaper. So one Monday, Mom sliced a little sliver of ham, put it and one bean on a butter chip and set it on the counter in front of the judge. He began to poke his fork all over the counter before he finally looked up from the paper and saw that Mother had pulled a joke on him.

Two blocks from the diner was an old

Around the Table

DINING DELIGHTS.
The Auburn Diner (below) was the place to eat around the Auburn, Indiana, courthouse in the '50s. Deanna Provines worked for her mother, who's shown in the center in the photo at left.

hotel. Four elderly men from the hotel also came in for lunch daily. If one of them didn't show up, I was sent to the hotel to see if he was ill. If the man was sick, I'd report his symptoms to my mother, and she'd fix up enough food to last him a couple of days.

Another "special" we prepared was for a regular customer who'd had all of his teeth pulled. While he waited for his dentures, we poured milk on his cornflakes and put them in the refrigerator to soften them.

The regular menu was ham and beans on Monday, and fish and macaroni and cheese on Friday. On other days, it might be beef and noodles, baked steak, roast pork and dressing, baked hash, meat loaf or sausage and sauerkraut.

Mom also baked seven pies every day but Sunday, when we closed at noon. Her pies were picture-perfect as well as delicious. The crusts were so good and flaky because they were made using lard.

No matter what Mom cooked, though, I never saw her use a recipe book.

Our most unusual customers came at the end of September during the annual street fair. Booths were set up all around the courthouse square and down side streets.

Sideshow at the Stools

During fair week, we opened an hour early, at 5 a.m. That's when workers from the sideshows came in to get their food for the day. They couldn't leave their shows during the hours people were paying to see them. I remember the alligator man, the ape woman, the fat lady and the three-legged man…and I never had to pay a cent.

The Court Theater was next to the diner. The very nice young man who took tickets there often came in for a ham sandwich. That nice young man became my husband in 1957.

The diner is long gone and the space is now a parking lot for the courthouse. But I still have my wonderful memories.

OUR FAVORITE GRACE

"My granddaughter was about 3 years old when she offered this prayer," shares Myrna Campbell, Guymon, Oklahoma. "Her mother had brought home take-out food, and as she set the bags on the table, Madison hopped into her chair, folded her hands, bowed her head and said:

Lord, thank you for the food, bless it and please make it a corn dog!

'Mom's' was the place for pies

By Ruberta Gorski, Daytona Beach, Florida

In the 1940s, my mother, Bertha Davis, ran Mom's Restaurant in Youngstown, New York.

The restaurant was about a mile from Fort Niagara, which became an induction center when World War II started. We served many soldiers when they could get off base at night and on weekends.

All of our family worked at the restaurant. Dad was a good cook, and when he wasn't in the kitchen, he was busy cutting hair in his barbershop next door, in the same building.

We needed all the help we could get on weekends when the soldiers came in. Sometimes they would be three deep at the counter waiting for their banana splits and milk shakes.

The soldiers were especially fond of our homemade pies. My sister Rita started baking pies when she was only 15. She even sold some at a small bake shop before the restaurant was opened. Two of the favorites were apple and banana cream.

A FAMILY AFFAIR. "In this 1942 photo, I'm sitting on the right side of the booth," says Ruberta Gorski. "My sister Ruth Hoolihan is sitting on the left side of the booth, holding her young daughter, Merrily.

"Our mother, Bertha Davis, is shown behind the cash register. My sister Bertha is the next one down the counter. The woman next to her is a soldier's wife who worked at the restaurant. Next to her is Nora Lee Johnson, who grew up in Youngstown.

"My father, Rubert, can be seen in the serving window."

Dining Out Adventures

diners were a delight

Casual comfort had the feel of home...but with more fun.

Tykes and Trikes Welcome

In 1952, my mother, Dorothy Blackburn (above, far right), worked at Ted and Marie's Diner in Covington, Tennessee. Ted and Marie (behind the counter) lived in the back of the diner with their daughter Eva Lynn (on the stool, right).

One day, my mother took me (on the stool, left) with her to pick up her paycheck. That's when I met Eva Lynn. We were both 4 years old and got along so well that Ted and Marie asked my mother to bring me with her to work so Eva Lynn and I could play.

We had so much fun that we cried at the end of the day when I had to go home.

—*Brenda McCaleb, Nashville, Tennessee*

OME OF
e **Big Boy**
E ORIGINAL
UBLE DECK
mburger

Bob's

amous
or
CHILI
· **STEAKS**
· **THICK
SHAKES**

old fashioned
PANCAKES

© 1949

Some people think
a balanced diet is
a burger in each hand.

BIG HANGOUT.
"I was raised in Glendale, California, home of the original Big Boy drive-in restaurant," says Stan Hendrickson of San Clemente. "In the '50s, we loved the burgers and malts and watching the girls and cars there."

IS EVERYBODY HAPPY? The Every Bodies Lunch diner in Palmyra, Pennsylvania, was owned and operated by my parents, Harry and Helen "Curly" Shutter. Their "fast food" restaurant was famous for its barbecues, hot dogs and Mother's homemade pies. That's my mother behind the counter in 1929. In the '50s, my parents opened Shutter's Superior Potato Chips in Hershey, Pennsylvania.

—*Janet Semeraro, Clinton, New York*

let's stop at HoJo's

Postwar travel boom put Howard Johnson's restaurants on the map.

Misses That Food

What I wouldn't give to eat at a Howard Johnson's again! I remember the orange-and-turquoise buildings from my youth.

I usually got the fried clams. The tartar sauce was so good, and they put a whole glass pot filled with it on the table. I even used the sauce on my french fries.

My family stayed at many Howard Johnson's Motor Lodges during vacations, and I don't think we ever got tired of the food there. It was so nice to walk right next door to a place where you knew the food would be good.

—*Gail Molnar, Shelby Township, Michigan*

"Newly Wed" Was Plain to See

As my new husband and I headed out for our honeymoon in New York City, we stopped at a Howard Johnson's Motor Lodge in New Jersey.

After checking into the lodge, we went into the restaurant. There I was, sitting at the table in my going-away dress and a corsage pinned to my outfit. How embarrassed I was when the waitress asked me if I was just married. I was 18 years old and must have had "new bride" written all over my face!

Years later, my husband and I took our five youngsters to HoJo's every once in a while for ice cream sundaes. My favorite was hot fudge.

—*Arline Benes Nenni*
Goffstown, New Hampshire

They Made the *Best*

Ah, the open highway, an orange roof ahead and time to stop and eat. Could this be a beautiful dream?

When I was young, we made at least two trips a year to visit relatives. The Pennsylvania Turnpike was pretty, but most important, it had several Howard Johnson's rest stops.

My greatest HoJo's memory is their wonderful hot dogs. They baked their own buns, then made a slice down instead of across, buttered and toasted the slice, put in a grilled hot dog and ketchup and put it all in a cardboard boat.

I've been a coast-to-coast nomad since high school and haven't yet found a hot dog to even match Howard Johnson's.

—*William Oglethorpe*
Alamogordo, New Mexico

Perfect for a Sunday Drive

I was born and raised in Altoona, Pennsylvania, near the original Pennsylvania Turnpike.

Taking the turnpike was not an advantage for us because it took us out of our way, but we'd go on Sunday afternoons, have dinner, then return on another route.

My favorite meal was beef potpie—a simple bowl of beef stew baked in a pie crust, always nicely browned. This came with a dinner roll and small salad, and a dish of HoJo's ice cream for dessert.

I got vanilla or chocolate, but my family would experiment with other flavors, like black walnut, butter pecan or pistachio.

A unique thing about the Midway Plaza, where we ate, was that the restaurant was on the eastbound side of the turnpike. The dining room was large, and the gift shop was loaded with goodies. But westbound travelers could park their cars on the other side and go through a pedestrian tunnel to get to the restaurant and do some shopping.

They've since closed the tunnel and have fast-food restaurants on both sides of the turnpike, but I'll never forget our Sunday meals.

—*John Grimme*
Columbus, Ohio

 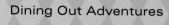

that first restaurant meal was the best

Mom & Dad had an extra-special treat for the whole family in the early '60s.

By Venita Buneta, Springfield, Missouri

We didn't pinch pennies in our house when I was growing up in Lacoochee, Florida. We squeezed them until they cried!

My parents both had full-time jobs, sometimes two, just to feed us six kids and keep a roof over our heads.

Still, they managed to save enough so that we could all go to an amusement park every year.

We'd eat breakfast early, hop in the station wagon and head out to Six Gun Territory.

That day was wonderful, seeing the sights and riding the rides.

Our stomachs settled only long enough to beg for a soft drink, cotton candy or popcorn. The treats were barely swallowed when we'd run off for more fun.

Parking Lot Picnics

Lunch was a sandwich in the parking lot, then back inside. When the shadows lengthened, we knew time was running out, although we were never ready to leave.

When it was time to go, there was another quick sandwich in the parking lot before we piled in the station wagon for the trip home.

The world seemed a little better, a little more special after that. My brothers and sisters and I even argued a little less…for a few days, anyway.

One year, however, there was a difference. We'd enjoyed a wonderful day at the park, and when it was time to go, we gathered around the station wagon, expecting the usual sandwich, when Mom spoke.

"We're going to a restaurant," she said.

Restaurants Were a Rare Treat

Stunned silence greeted this announcement. We never went to a restaurant. Money was too dear and there were too many of us.

But Mom had said it and that meant it was so. We all piled into the car, anticipation making our mouths water.

The restaurant served burgers and steaks, and the aroma hit us before we got out of the car. With stomachs growling, we entered the restaurant slowly and quietly.

The waitress put some tables together, and we all sat down.

"Order whatever you like," Dad said magnanimously as my parents smiled, happy they could do this.

I know Mom and Dad thought we'd order burgers, like most kids. But we didn't. All of us, right down to the last one, wanted steak. We'd never had steaks, though we'd tasted burgers on rare occasions.

Mom and Dad ducked behind the menu and conferred briefly. Their smiling faces appeared.

"You can all have steak," Dad said.

"But it's a long drive home, so only water to drink," Mom added.

When the waitress took our orders, Mom said

> **When it comes to restaurants, the lower the lights the higher the prices.**

she and Dad were still full from lunch and wouldn't be eating.

They smiled while we had delicious salads. They chatted with each of us about our grand day while we slathered ketchup on our French fries.

Mom helped most of us cut up our steaks and didn't take a bite, even when some of us offered.

We all agreed it was the best meal we'd ever eaten—except that if Mom cooked it, it would have been even better. Mom liked that part.

We finished every last bite, including the parsley garnishes, wiped our mouths, pushed our chairs back and smiled.

Our parents looked very satisfied as we all climbed into the station wagon.

We thanked them again before settling down for the trip home.

I sleepily watched as Mom snuggled against Dad. Then I heard her whisper to him, "Life doesn't get any better than this."

Dad looked away from the road long enough to gently kiss Mom on her forehead.

As my eyes closed, I remember thinking that this was simply the best day ever!

Patrons Paid with Honor

When my grandparents operated their restaurant in Baltimore's business district and inner harbor area, their customers paid by the honor system.

George and Henrietta Kuehnl opened the restaurant on Pratt Street in 1900, serving and selling food in the traditional way. When World War I caused a labor shortage, they decided to try something else.

Customers ordered food at the bar, enjoyed their meal, then told the cashier how much they owed and paid up.

In the early days, the restaurant served three meals a day and opened at 4 a.m. For many years, my grandparents lived in an apartment above the restaurant.

Because of the large factories nearby, many prominent businessmen came for lunches that sometimes lasted a couple of hours. The tables were covered with white linens and the waiters wore white gloves to serve such dishes as crab cakes, fried oysters and homemade baked goods.

The restaurant closed in 1970 and was later razed for the Orioles' new stadium. It was the last "honor system" restaurant in the city.
—*Frederick Kuehnl*
Selbyville, Delaware

ON MY HONOR. Before Kuehnl's began its honor system, they had white-gloved waiters. In this early 1900s photo above, "Pop" Kuehnl, as he was known to customers, can be seen at far right behind the counter.

Woolworth's made memories for many

5-and-10-cent store was the best in town.

Biggest and Best

While I was growing up in the '50s, my mom worked at Woolworth's in downtown Grand Rapids, Michigan. My father had passed away, so Mom had to work outside the home.

On Friday evenings when she had to work, we kids hopped on the bus to go downtown and have supper with her. It was truly the highlight of our week. I always ordered macaroni and cheese. It was the best tasting and biggest serving.

I'm sure the lady who served us knew that we had very little, so she always gave me an extra spoonful.

—*Peg Perry, Waukesha, Wisconsin*

Don't Mind Us

When my mother and I took the streetcar to Minneapolis to shop in the '30s and '40s, we always headed for Woolworth's lunch counter at noon.

By this time, the counter's swivel seats were usually all occupied, so we checked the seated diners to determine who would finish eating first. Then we stood right behind those seats until the people left and we could sit down.

No one seemed to be rushed by this custom, and once we were served, it wasn't long before someone was standing right behind us, waiting their turn.

—*Alice Stoesz, Coon Rapids, Minnesota*

Be Careful at Lunch

When my mother, twin sister and I left our farm for a major shopping trip to Albert Lea, Minnesota, we always included a trip to F.W. Woolworth for lunch.

A favorite item was a bacon, lettuce and tomato club sandwich. Our homemade sandwiches looked nothing like those masterpieces. We also liked their flaky, plump baked apple dumplings with vanilla sauce.

On one trip, I noticed large black and white signs posted on the tile walls. Worried,

FIRST JOB. "When I was 16, back in 1942, I got my first job—as a cashier at the Woolworth's store in Chicago," writes Eleanor Soukup Bara of Palos Hills, Illinois. "In the picture (opposite), I'm in the back row behind the manager's left shoulder."

I pointed at them and asked Mother what they would do to me if I spilled.

She read the signs, then explained to me that "No Tipping" had nothing to do with spilling a beverage at the lunch counter.

I enjoyed my lunch so much more knowing that even if I spilled, I could still come back.

—*Jean Collins, Eden Prairie, Minnesota*

Laying It on Pretty Thick

Growing up in upper Manhattan in the '30s and '40s, I often went with my mother to the Woolworth's in Washington Heights.

Over the lunch counter was a big sign with red letters that said, "The Drink You Eat With A Spoon!" My mother bought me my first milk shake there. It came in a tall paper cup with a long spoon and tasted so good, I thought I was in heaven.

I just couldn't get over that wording, "The Drink You Eat With A Spoon!" It intrigued me.

A few years later, when I started going to Woolworth's by myself, it dawned on me that the

drink was merely a very thick milk shake.

But it was still good, and even today I order a milk shake extra thick and think of those times at Woolworth's with my mother.

—*Carol Costa Jarrel, Duluth, Georgia*

Shake a Leg for Lunch

There were hundreds of restaurants I could have chosen for lunch when I worked for a large insurance company in downtown St. Paul, Minnesota.

But I always chose the Woolworth lunch counter. It was my favorite place, as that's where my grandmother took me when I was a little girl in Minneapolis.

I remember the lunch counter was next to the hosiery counter. It made me chuckle to look up from my lunch and see those rows of nylon-stockinged, upturned plastic legs. No other restaurant since has met that level of ambience.

—*Lee Ann Gustafson, Edina, Minnesota*

OUR FAVORITE GRACE

"*When our sons were small, this was their favorite grace,*" says Clara DeCaro, Lehigh Acres, Florida.

Our health is given by this food; our food, dear Lord, comes by Thy grace. Our thanks we offer in return at every meal, in every place.

Mom-and-pop ice cream parlor was her Mom and Pop's

Homemade ice cream, jukebox music and dancing in the aisles made a Brooklyn ice cream parlor popular.

By Marilyn Peterson, Sebastian, Florida

My father, Herman August Frederick Dodenhoff, came to America in 1922, when he was 18. He became known as "Gus," served in the Army as a cook during World War II, then bought an ice cream parlor after his discharge.

My brother, Ron, and I practically grew up in the parlor, which was located in the Bay Ridge section of Brooklyn, New York.

Dad had the perfect personality to own a business where he dealt with customers.

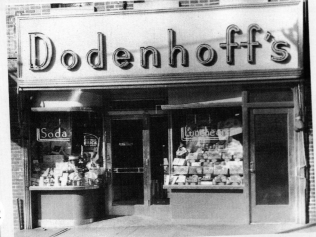

Teenagers came in to relax with a Coke before going home to do their homework. They played the jukebox and even danced.

Dad didn't mind, although if anyone got too rowdy, he would nicely ask them to leave. Everyone knew Dad never held a grudge and would welcome them back.

The ice cream parlor was open six days a week, but that didn't mean Dad rested on Sunday. That was the day he made the ice cream using natural ingredients. It spoiled me, and I don't eat the ice cream made today.

My mother, Helen, was key to the success of the business. When Dad made chocolate turkeys for Thanksgiving, or bunnies and baskets for Easter, Mom decorated them. She also decorated his ice cream cakes.

Mom had a full-time job as a secretary during the day and worked in the store at night.

When it got busy, I washed dishes and Ron waited on customers.

But it was Dad who was in the store all the time, so he was seldom able to come to my school plays and dance recitals.

Still, he was always there to talk to, confide in and lean on. I was his little girl even after I had married and had my own children.

When Dad died in 1984, I felt I had lost part of my own heart and soul. But memories of him and the ice cream parlor remain.

ice cream sunday

On Sunday afternoons, while I was growing up in rural
West Bend, Wisconsin, a special treat for me and
my two sisters was a stop at Kuesters Tavern with
Mama and Daddy. We were always on our best behavior
and thus rewarded with an extra-large ice cream cone.

—Brad Kemp, Tucson, Arizona

HOWELL WALKER/NATIONAL GEOGRAPHIC SOCIETY/CORBIS

CHAPTER SIX

We Never Went Hungry

While most of us are fortunate these days to have more than enough food on our plates, that wasn't always the case. From tough times during the Depression to rationing during World War II, it took hard work, determination and, oftentimes, creativity to feed a hungry family.

"Mama went to great lengths to provide for our family of nine," recalls Sylvia Brownstein of Bronx, New York. "To stretch meals as much as she could, she cut chicken into little parts and put them into a huge cooking pot with onions, garlic, carrots, celery, green peas and string beans. It cooked for hours.

"After smelling the wonderful aroma of the simmering supper for hours, we finally feasted on delicious chicken soup and chicken. Mama always ate the chicken feet, so I thought that was the part she liked. As the years went by, I realized that the feet were the only parts left for her. Mama sacrificed so the rest of the family could have their fill."

Read on for more inspiring stories of how families were kept nourished during trying times…

HOW DO YOU STRETCH
A 12-POUND TURKEY
TO FEED MORE THAN
20 GUESTS? THIS
DEPRESSION-ERA MOM
KNEW THE TRICK!

mom made a feast from
a famished bird

By Bill Livingstone
Santa Barbara, California

On Thanksgiving Day 1933, in the depths of the Great Depression, a lot of guests came to our house at 63rd and Alviso in southwest Los Angeles. Grandma, Grandpa, aunts, uncles and cousins joined us for dinner.

There were over 20 people, and the turkey my mom was roasting began to look mighty small.

Out in the kitchen, Mom and her sisters were preparing the holiday dinner. Aunt Hattie basted the bird and said to Mom, "Rachel, I guess we're lucky to be able to afford this turkey. But he's such a little bird, I'm afraid there won't be enough for everyone."

"Well," Aunt Cecil said thoughtfully as she mashed the potatoes, "we have many things to be thankful for. We're all well and we're all together."

My creative Aunt Mary offered a suggestion. "The kitchen crew could say we ate some of the turkey before it left the kitchen," she said with a sly grin.

"Don't worry," assured Mom, as she made gravy. "I have a plan. Everyone will have all the turkey they want."

My dear grandmother, who had baked a half dozen pumpkin pies for the get-together, shook her head and laughed, "Sometimes I worry about you, Rachel. How are you going to satisfy a dozen hungry kids and 10 adults with one skinny 12-pound bird?"

Mom Had a Plan

Mom just smiled and gave a wink.

Then my bachelor Uncle Arnold, with his balding head and friendly face, came into the kitchen and put a bottle of bootleg wine in the icebox. (Prohibition was repealed the next month.)

"I hope there's plenty of food," he said.

CHEAPER BY THE DOZEN. When Bill Livingstone's family gathered for a holiday, planning the menu took a genius. In this photo, taken on Christmas 1929, Bill's standing at far right in front of his parents, wearing a cowboy outfit.

"I could eat a horse."

"I wish we had a horse to feed you," Aunt Hattie laughed. "Then there'd be more turkey for the rest of us."

Our dining room couldn't handle anywhere near the number of relatives who were there for Thanksgiving dinner, so we did what we always did when the whole family got together—the kids ate

> *We went through that pie like Roosevelt went through Hoover in the recent election.*

first. When they were done and cleared out, the adults sat down.

By the time dinner was ready, we kids had been outside running around and worked up an appetite. Mom stepped out onto the front porch and called us. "Come on and wash up. It's time to eat!"

We cleaned up quickly and all rushed for a place at the table, with no more than the usual amount of pushing and poking. Mom was about to pull off what is now known as the "Great Turkey Caper," and we never knew a thing about it.

I'll never forget her angelic smile as Mom stepped through the double-swinging kitchen door and asked, "How many kids want pumpkin pie first?"

Of course, every hand immediately went up! To whoops of delight, my aunts marched in with plates of Grandma's sweet pumpkin pie.

We went through that pie like Roosevelt went through Hoover in the recent election. Then Mom came through the door again and asked, "Anyone want more pie?"

Again every hand went up, and more pie went down. But toward the end of that second piece, we slowed down. Suddenly, we all felt very full.

Then Mom came through the swinging door for the third time. "Anyone want more pumpkin pie?" This time there were no takers. "OK," Mom said, still smiling, "how many want some turkey now?"

With our bellies full of Grandma's pumpkin pie, not a single hand went up.

"All right," said Mom, her voice now with some authority. "Kids out of the dining…adults in."

The adults, of course, had all the turkey they could hold.

For years afterward, anytime the family got together, we all laughed at Mom's genius in stretching that Depression turkey to feed 22 people.

Life is short— eat dessert first.

Dad Had Us See Humor in Monotonous Meal

In a time when most people were just trying to survive, our dad's wonderful sense of humor got us through.

When Dad was laid off, Mom found work, but the meager pay left little money for food. Dad was determined not to go on welfare, and Mom agreed. He did all the cooking. Once we had potatoes three days in a row.

While setting the table, I put out a bowl for the potatoes, but Dad told me to put out two more. I excitedly told my brother, "We're going to have more than potatoes tonight. Dad told me to put out three bowls!" We could hardly wait for Mom to get home so we could eat.

But when we sat down, each bowl was filled with potatoes. Dad passed one around, saying, "Have some roast beef." Then he passed another, saying, "Try some of these delicious string beans. Would you like some corn? Oh, yes…and do have some potatoes."

We all got to laughing and joined in the game, passing bowls back and forth, pretending each one held a different food.

—*Evelyn Robinson, South Bend, Indiana*

OUR FAVORITE GRACE

"Some special friends shared this prayer with us many years ago," says Julie Stein from Libertyville, Illinois. *"It's simple but meaningful."*

Some people in the world are hungry and have no food. Some people in the world are lonely and have no friends. Thank you, God, we have both.

mush didn't cut it

Industrious kids came up with a plan to add variety to their breakfasts during the Depression.

By Robert Stover, West Allis, Wisconsin

In 1937 and '38, times were pretty hard for many people. My mother, sister, grandmother and I were living together in Battle Creek, Michigan, in a small two-bedroom house for $12 a month.

That sounds like low-cost housing, but my mother took in neighbors' washing and ironing—in addition to her regular job at a tent and awning shop—just to pay the rent.

We were on relief, known today as welfare. That provided us with some of the basic foods and vegetables in season, including white cornmeal called mush.

Each Saturday morning, my sister and I walked across town to pay our weekly visit to these two cereal giants.

Mom cooked this for breakfast. After it set, the leftover mush was cut into slices and fried up for a later meal.

Since we got tired of mush, my sister and I figured out how to get a better variety of breakfast food.

Both Kellogg's and Post Cereal were located in Battle Creek, about a quarter mile apart and not too far from our house. Each Saturday morning, my sister and I walked across town to pay our weekly visit to these two cereal giants. Both companies conducted tours of their plants, and at the end of the Kellogg's tour, visitors were given six small sample boxes of cereal. I think they're better known now as variety packs.

After the tour, we were also served a small dish of ice cream in their cafeteria, which was a real treat.

Next Stop: Post

When we left Kellogg's, we'd walk over to Post and hide our Kellogg's cereal in the bushes before taking the Post tour. At the end of that tour, we received a gift package of Post cereals, plus a sample of Postum, an instant drink served as an alternative to coffee or tea, which we didn't like.

We'd then retrieve our Kellogg's cereal and go home with a week's supply.

After about eight weekly visits to these plants, we became well known. So well, in fact, that the tour guides just smiled and said, "Here, kids. You don't have to take the tour if you don't want to."

They'd just give us ice cream and the cereal and say, "Bye. See you next week."

What wonderful people to meet during hard times! It made life a little easier.

we picked potatoes by moonlight

Gleaning spuds from a field in the dark put them between some rocks and a hard place.

By Douglas West, Baldwinsville, New York

I realize we were "different" from most families when I think about the potato fields near our home in Palermo, New York.

I was the oldest of eight kids, and Mom worked hard to raise us. Dad was gone, sometimes for weeks, working construction. I know we were poor, but it didn't seem like we had hard times. As kids, what did we know?

There was that day, though when Mom told us we were going to pick potatoes.

It was the end of the season and a machine had already gone through the fields, but there were still plenty of potatoes left on the ground.

Those leftovers would have been plowed under the next day, anyway, but Mom was too proud to ask the farmer if we could take them. Her plan was to pick the potatoes that night!

Put the Plan in Motion

Mom spent the day telling us it was going to be so much fun. And the rewards would be many—french fries, potato chips, baked

potatoes, mashed potatoes.

We put the youngest kids to bed early, then made beds in back of the station wagon so they could sleep while the rest of us worked.

Around 10 p.m., we woke everyone up. Along with the family dog and a stack of burlap bags, we piled into the station wagon.

We sang along with the radio for the short ride, and when Mom found the field, she pulled

> ## And the rewards would be many—french fries, potato chips, baked potatoes, mashed potatoes.

way off the road and parked.

We tied the dog to the bumper to guard the car and walked into the field.

The moon was up, but the ground was dark with shadows. The potato picker had left deep trenches, and we couldn't even see our feet, much less the potatoes. We worked most of the night by feeling for our treasure.

There sure seemed to be lots of potatoes. Every now and then we'd find one that had been chopped up by the machine and throw it at the nearest kid. There was a lot of giggling and snickering. We whispered, but kind of

TATER TOTS OR ROCK HOUNDS? Douglas West is surrounded by five of his sisters in this Christmas picture from the '60s.

loudly, and when someone would go "Pssst!" we'd look around to see who'd done it and start giggling all over again.

When I had my bag filled about halfway, I went over to one of the girls, dumped her bag in mine and headed back to the station wagon for another bag.

Just then a car came down the road. We all looked at Mom, who dove to the ground so as not to be seen. We did the same but were giggling at the way she flopped down.

After about three hours, I had made numerous trips to the wagon with full bags. We were tired and grubby. The little ones were crying.

"That's enough," Mom said. "Grab what you've got and let's go make some midnight potato chips!"

We scrambled back to the car. By the time all the potato sacks were loaded, the rear bumper was almost touching the ground.

The sacks were spread out to even the load and we crawled on top of them. We sat so high, we couldn't see out the windows. Every time we hit a dip in the road, the bumper would

scrape and sparks flew up.

Back home, Mom told the kids to get cleaned up while she peeled some potatoes and got the grease hot for the chips. Then we dragged in a couple of sacks and dumped them on the kitchen floor.

Mom pawed through the pile, then sat down on the floor and started to cry.

You see, most of the potatoes we gathered in the dark were really dirt-covered rocks!

We all felt so bad for her. We dragged in more bags to sort through, but every single one was more than half full of rocks.

To this day, I'll bet that house still has rocks edging the driveway, the walkway and the flower garden. Every bush and tree was ringed with rocks.

I've always imagined that the people who lived there after us said, "I wonder where they got all of these rocks."

days of rationing didn't dampen spirits

During World War II, folks on the home front went without to help men and women overseas fight their battles.

Neighbors Came Through

Although I was only a child during World War II, one memory of those days remains vivid.

My younger brother, Robert, was just 3 in 1944. He had been very ill, first with a kidney disease and then with pneumonia. (That's me and Robert in the photo below.)

When Robert came home from the hospital, he was very weak. The doctor was able to get extra meat rations for Robert to build up his strength.

But that didn't mean our mother was always able to find meat at the grocery stores near our home in Dallas, Texas.

So our neighbors all pitched in. Whenever they had meat, they would save a small portion for Robert and send it over to our house.

Their caring and willingness to share made a strong impression on me.

—Margaret Johnson
Bartlesville, Oklahoma

School of Hard Knocks

I was attending a small Bible institute in 1944. Because of rationing, the school could not buy granulated sugar, only sugar cubes.

We students had to have sugar on our cereal. So we'd place a sugar cube on the back of a metal folding chair, grasp a knife by the blade and whack the cube with the handle.

I can still hear the racket through the dining hall as we turned our sugar from cubes to granulated!

—Gordon Preiser, Eustis, Florida

Desire for a Good Dinner Led to Bartering

My dad was a meat-and-potatoes man and was determined to have his meat in spite of rationing. I was an only child, and we didn't use all of our canned goods coupons, so my mother traded with an aunt, who had eight children and couldn't afford much meat.

Sugar stamps were traded to a neighbor whose boys each had a sweet tooth and loaded their coffee with sugar.

We only used our car for going to church or the grocery store, so we were able to trade gasoline stamps to families who needed to drive more.

After all that creative bartering, Dad got to enjoy his favorite meal!

—Marcella Clark, Rocky River, Ohio

Rationing Didn't Stop Wedding Feast

This 1945 photo (above) shows my new wife, Mary, and me at our Italian-style wedding in Chicago. Over 1,000 guests feasted on roast beef and sausage sandwiches, plus an abundance of Italian pastries and cannoli. Sugar was still rationed, so family members and friends donated their sugar stamps.

I had just returned from the service, and Mother insisted that we have this elaborate cake. The arch is artificial but frosted, and on top of that are three sheet cakes. Stacked cakes on either side created the columns.

—Sam Cipolla, *Pleasant Prairie, Wisconsin*

A pessimist is the only one who sees the hole in the doughnut.

Had a Flair with Flank

During World War II, flank steak was just about the only meat people could buy without red meat tokens. It only cost 10 cents for an entire steak.

The butcher didn't believe that I was buying it for my husband and me to eat, rather than a treat for the dog, since flank steak was the toughest steak in his counter.

I told him how I prepared it...rolled around stuffing, tied with a string and sliced crosswise when done.

The very next time I went to buy a flank steak, he said I needed meat tokens, and he'd raised the price to 35 cents per steak!

—*Iola Headlee, Midvale, Utah*

Thumbs-up for Mom

Butter was rare at our A&P store on Flatbush Avenue in Brooklyn during World War II.

When the word went out in the neighborhood that there was butter in the store, I was given the cash and the ration coupons and sent to get a pound. Back then, butter was scooped out of a tub like ice cream.

After standing in a long line for service, I triumphantly went home and handed the butter over to my mother. She promptly weighed it on a balance scale and had to add a silver knife to equal a pound.

Much to my chagrin, she made me take it back to the store, together with the knife, and tell the man to "keep his thumb off the scale this time."

I did as I was told, but it was small consolation to this 12-year-old kid when I got a round of applause from the customers in line.

—*Adele Ritchie Gatens*
Fanwood, New Jersey

The Fudge Factor

Chocolate fudge was a great childhood delight, but with sugar being rationed, that treat was out of the question.

Every summer, our small New Hampshire town had a street fair. One of the games was bingo, and among the prizes was a five-pound bag of sugar. I was only 9 or 10 years old, but I finally won a game. I quickly extracted a promise from my mother that she would make fudge if I took the sugar.

She did, and never has fudge tasted better.

—*Shirley Wentworth, Alexandria, Virginia*

OUR FAVORITE GRACE

"This was and still is our family's grace. When the four of us were kids and we were really hungry, this prayer was offered so quickly that only God would have known what was said," relates Joanne Melling of Victoria, British Columbia.

God bless this food which we now take and do us good for Jesus' sake. Amen.

"Can <u>your</u> food bills be cut? *SURE!*"

"Believe me, 'shopping around' isn't the easiest or quickest way to lower weekly food bills—though lots of women think so. It may surprise you, as it did me, that A&P, the store that *really can* lower your food bills, doesn't believe in 'hit-or-miss' values. They say everyone is entitled to low prices, all through the store, every day . . . *that* saves you more money in the long run. That makes sense to me . . . and my food bills prove it's right."

Reducing the weekly food bills of A&P customers is accomplished by our consistently low prices . . . every day on hundreds of items. It can't be done with just a few "occasional" values.

Millions of quality-wise, economy-con-scious homemakers evidently agree that we have the right idea—because more of them shop at thrifty A&P Super Markets today than ever before. If stretching your food budget is a problem . . . or if you feel your food bills are too high, A&P's money-saving policy of "low prices every day for everyone," can help you spend less—and eat better!

HOLIDAY FOODS AT EVERY DAY LOW PRICES

Come to your A&P Super Market for fancy holiday fare . . . fine fruit and vegetables . . . crunchy nuts, candies . . . choice cheeses . . . Super-Right meats and plump poultry. Like everything else at A&P these festive foods are sold at every day low prices. Come see!

NO "GUESS WORK" HERE

You'll find that A&P's every day low prices are stamped right on every can, package, jar and bottle in the store. No question what you're paying with A&P's "Accurate Price Marking." And it means faster service at the check-out counter . . . easier checking when you're home. You'll like it!

MORE FOOD FOR YOUR MONEY

Feeding a healthy, growing family is no easy chore these days—particularly with a limited budget. S-T-R-E-T-C-H your food dollars by shopping at A&P where only *about 1 cent* of every dollar you spend is net profit to A&P. It means more for your money!

Customers' Corner

Come shop at an A&P Super Market. See if our every day low prices don't help your budget. Then write and tell us frankly just what you think of it. We're always happy to have your complaints or suggestions as to how we may serve you better.

Customer Relations Dept., A&P FOOD STORES
Graybar Building, New York 17, N. Y.

A&P SUPER MARKETS

1950

we may have been poor, but we had plenty of food

By Floyd Hedge, Mountain Home, Arkansas

In 1934, when I was boy of 12, my mom and dad and I moved in with my grandma in the southern-Illinois town of Albion.

The Depression was in full swing in that little town, and jobs were as scarce as diamonds in a coal mine. Dad was between jobs, and we had to go on government relief until we got back on our feet.

> *Dad used to joke that we were so poor, the flies had to carry a lunch when they came to our house!*

We never had any luxuries like electricity, a furnace, air-conditioning or even an electric fan. I did my homework at night by the light of a kerosene lamp. Dad used to joke that we were so poor, the flies had to carry a lunch when they came to our house!

But we had a big potbellied stove to keep us warm, plenty of homemade quilts to snuggle under at night and lots of good, wholesome food to eat.

My step-grandfather grew tobacco and had a big garden and several fruit trees. It was my job to pick the fruit and vegetables, and then Mom and Grandma slaved over a hot stove all summer to can them and make jams and jellies for the coming winter.

I especially remember the huge platters of fried bread that Grandma made for supper every night, along with the ever-present pot of great northern beans and a No. 10 cast-iron skillet that was filled with fried potatoes.

I always finished off my meal with peanut butter mixed with either a half-pint of blackberry jam, peach preserves or sorghum molasses.

We ate a lot of inexpensive meat back then: a steak probably would have made us sick! We had a lot of jowl meat, salt pork and liver—cuts of meat that "better offs" didn't want. And we were glad to get it.

On rare occasions, we had what Dad called "Hoover ham" (baloney) along with cheddar cheese and crackers.

When President Roosevelt started the WPA, Dad was lucky enough to get a job for a dollar a day running the wooden end of a long-handled shovel used to grade ditch banks.

After that, we were able to rent a house of our own, but those earlier recollections will have a special place in my mind forever.

> The secret to contentment is to settle for half a measure before the cup runs over and makes a mess.

fishing put food on the table

By Mabel Zelenka, Griffin, Georgia

During the Depression, my family was lucky to live on Long Island, with access to the local creeks and bays. There was no pollution then, and the waterfront was not as popular. Anyone who was ambitious could find plenty of clams, eels, mussels, scallops and crabs.

Digging for clams was an all-day job if you had the right equipment, but few of us had anything fancy. We had to wait for the tide to go out, when the sandbars were bare. Almost all our fishing was done by hand or with nets.

We caught eels mostly at night, using spears. It was hard work, but fulfilling if you liked eels. Fishing wasn't a pastime for us—it was food on the table.

On Sundays, we'd drive to farms on the island to stock up on vegetables. With plenty of food from the farms and the bay, we didn't need much money. We worked hard, but we enjoyed life, too.

INDUSTRIOUS ISLANDER. Mabel Zelenka (above left) and fellow Long Islanders harvested clams, eels, mussels and more from creeks and bays. Many of her neighbors lived in beachfront cottages like the one above right.

seasons determined many families' menus

No frills foods were still fantastic.

By Juanita Killough Urbach, Brush, Colorado

Our eating habits in the 1930s were regulated by the seasons. The grocery bill always had to be kept to a minimum because our only reliable source of income came from selling eggs and cream.

We welcomed spring each year. It was a time of hope. We searched the fence corners for lamb's-quarters, added winter onions to our scrambled eggs and pulled tender rhubarb shoots for pies.

bushels of peaches and pears for canning. Baskets of grapes were bought for jelly. Potatoes, carrots and onions were dug up and stored in the cellar.

Winter was soup season. A meaty bone boiled with vegetables made a tasty appetizer. Thicker, meatier stews were meals in themselves. Chicken noodle soup was a favorite, as were potato soup, and navy bean soup with bits of ham or bacon.

Tomato soup was a Depression

Food preparation required more work then, but the cooks were creative. If they were out of one ingredient, they substituted another.

Soon there would be leaf lettuce, radishes and green onions from the garden. Topped with a sweet-and-sour cream dressing, they would become tasty salads.

The meat supply would be running low as spring approached, so whatever we had left was alternated with stewing hens.

In summertime, since we had no refrigeration, we cooked only enough food for one meal. Excess vegetables were preserved in a variety of ways. Green beans and tomatoes were canned. Sweet corn was cut from the cob and spread on a white sheet to dry. Cabbage was shredded and put into stone jars with salt for sauerkraut.

When fall came, we bought a few

specialty. Home-canned tomatoes and milk were heated separately, and a little soda was added to the tomatoes to keep the milk from curdling when the two were combined. It had a unique flavor unmatched by any other tomato soup.

Food preparation required more work then, but the cooks were creative. If they were out of one ingredient, they substituted another: Flour replaced cornstarch, honey or syrup took the place of sugar, and baking soda and powder were used interchangeably. The changes were rarely detected, and the food was just as delicious and filling.

We might have felt poor during the Depression, but we ate like kings!

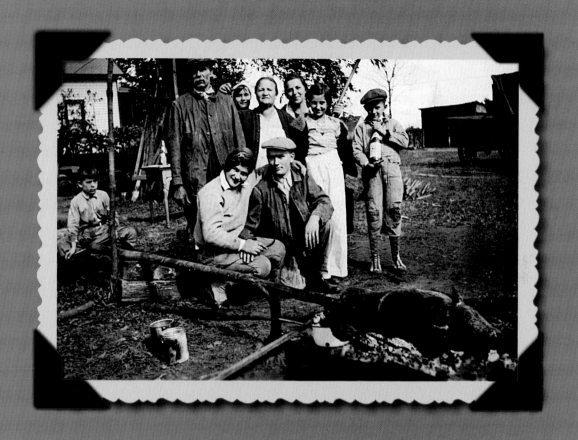

barbecue better than bread

In the middle of the Depression, the grocery stores in central New Jersey sold loaves of bread for a nickel. But even at that terrific price, store-bought bread was out of reach for our family of eight, so Mom spent plenty of time baking her own. Many times, bread was all we had to eat. In this photo, my family was lucky enough to have a pig roast. I'm turning the spit, and my parents are standing at left and third from the left.

—Tony Kostreba, Portales, New Mexico

CHAPTER SEVEN

Holiday Recollections

Never are traditions more treasured than during such holidays as Thanksgiving, Christmas and Easter. Whether your menu features the traditional, like turkey—or something more unconventional—the foods we enjoyed tasted like home.

"Over several years when I was growing up in the 1930s, our family and friends assembled, for all things, a Thanksgiving oyster roast," says Virginia Petersen from Raleigh, North Carolina.

"On Willoughby Beach, Virginia, we built a big fire. A wooden barrel full of oysters was placed on a sheet of metal sitting on poles over the fire.

"Since most of the children did not like oysters, hot dogs were also roasted on straightened coat hangers. Completing the meal would be deviled eggs, potato salad and baked beans.

"There was no joy like bundling up from the November cold and savoring the smell of salt air and roasting oysters and hot dogs."

Other folks share their own holiday customs on the pages that follow…

Thanksgiving
was a big family gathering

By Areldene Jenkins
Burton, Michigan

A peaceful and prosperous year made 1922 the perfect time for my great-uncle, Fred Tirrill, to stage a big family get-together for Thanksgiving at his home near Charlotte, Michigan.

His large brick house had been built with a long dining room to accommodate a table with all the leaves in place. True, his wife, Lou, had sighed when he mentioned the idea. Inviting Fred's brother, Judson, and his clan was no easy matter—everyone must be included.

When Lou totaled the family and then added in the hired people, the table had to be set for 30 guests. She started cooking and baking two weeks before.

We had snow early that year. As Papa drove up the gravel drive to the big brick house, he noticed the beauty of the huge front lawn, covered with an unbroken expanse of sparkling white snow.

As ministers often do, he had a sudden inspiration, although he didn't say a word.

At last, all the latecomers had arrived and everyone was seated at the huge table with lots of good-natured joshing. Father said a blessing, and the long-awaited passing of the serving dishes began.

Food in Abundance

It was a sumptuous spread that day, with a fat goose and a turkey with oyster stuffing. There were mashed potatoes with gravy and many succulent vegetables. Aunt Lou had baked a variety of breads, pies and cakes. The rich aroma of fresh coffee hung in the air.

The patriarchs, Uncle Fred and my grandfather, were stationed at the head of the table. They started carving and passing along platters of sliced meat and stuffing.

As the hot dishes moved around the table, conversation began to ripple around the big room.

The adults were all farmers or farmers'

AFTER-DINNER FROLIC. Before joining the clan in an after-dinner frolic, 9-year-old Areldene Jenkins posed for a picture with her sister, Alice Jo, mother, Nellie, and father, Maynard.

wives, and they loved these occasions when everyone gathered. Their ties were forged of times of laughter and tears. All belonged to a church, but this was their social life. They liked a good laugh and loved hearing about each other's lives and what had happened since they last met.

When everyone had as many helpings as possible of the main course, Aunt Lou and several of the women brought in the

The adults made more noise than any bunch of children we'd ever heard as we walked out to blue skies and pure white snow.

pies and plenty of fresh coffee. Most men refused fresh plates, insisting the pie tasted just as good on the big plate and it meant less dishes to wash.

Eternity is two people and a roasted turkey.

The pies, pumpkin and mince, vanished with alacrity, as everyone wanted two pieces.

Finally, sated and sleepy from food, everyone sat back to look at each other in the contentment that follows a holiday meal.

After a pause, my father pushed back his chair and stood up, tinkling a spoon against his glass.

"First of all, I want to thank Lou Tirrill for a truly glorious Thanksgiving dinner. We should all give her a hug and a kiss," he said.

"I see the children are all eager to be excused and run out in the snow to play. Well now, I suggest that we all put on our coats and join them for an hour of snow play. It will be a lively experience, and we will all feel better for it."

We children didn't think he would get anywhere with his proposition, but after much laughing and teasing, all the adults actually donned overshoes, hats and coats to go outdoors with us. Aunt Lou even left her kitchen chores and decided to join us like another child.

The adults made more noise than any bunch of children we'd ever heard as we all walked out to pretty blue skies and pure white snow.

A good time was had by all as, rosy-cheeked and packed with snow, we returned to the house, and we were swept off on the back porch.

One of Aunt Lou's sons had a camera, and now that I'm an octogenarian, I can hold the pictures from that day in my hand and hear again, as if from far off, the music of long-ago laughter and shouts.

It does not seem so very long since I was one of those hard-playing children. I have a strong nostalgia for a less complex and more peaceful time.

And, yes, I finally understand what is meant by the phrase "backbone of the country."

brighten the corner where you are

A simple hymn set the stage for a Thanksgiving revelation in 1934.

By Cora Owen, Wiscasset, Maine

Light gleamed cheerfully from behind the sparkling chimneys of oil lamps, driving the gloom from our shabby little kitchen. It revealed a clean worn floor bare of any covering, unpainted woodwork and walls lacking either paper or paint.

Mother, busy at the black iron stove where a wood fire snapped and crackled, prepared a meager supper for her family.

We four children were gathered around the table on that Sunday night in late November 1934 to sing hymns. Poor in quality, we compensated with enthusiasm and volume.

Dad sat listening to our concert, discouragement and anxiety on his face. Unemployed and in poor health, he worried about the fast-approaching Thanksgiving Day and the fact that he had no special dinner for his family.

I had chosen to lead my volunteer choir in a rendition of *Brighten the Corner Where You Are*. My 10-year-old mind did not grasp the significance of my choice.

Suddenly, there was a knock at the door. We continued to sing loudly.

Daddy tried to hush us, but we kept singing, "Brighten the corner where you are, brighten the corner where you are…"

He opened the door to find a deacon from our church with his wife and several other people. Their arms were full of bags and boxes. We stopped in surprise. Dad invited them in, apologizing for our racket.

"Don't stop them, Tom, let them sing," Deacon Gray said kindly. "Since Thanksgiving is near, we thought you might be able to use a few extra things."

Those bundles contained our whole Thanksgiving dinner and many other food items. People who had little more than we did were willing to share with us.

Dad bowed his head and wept. His heart had been stirred by our song and overwhelmed by the kindness of those people. He prayed as he had not prayed in many months.

We children had brightened a corner of our home with our singing. And our friends and neighbors had made a bright corner in the community by their thoughtfulness.

Together, we brightened a corner of my father's troubled heart.

GRATEFUL FAMILY. Living in Five Islands, Maine, at the time of Cora Owen's inspirational memory were hymn-singing children (from left), Cora Mae, Tom, Irving and Mary Frances.

'take your time'

Besides a bountiful Thanksgiving feast in the 1920s, Mom served up a generous helping of maternal wisdom.

By Enid Maringer, Federal Way, Washington

My mother liberally spiced her speech with aphorisms—those word gems that contain the wisdom of the ages. For example, after every trip we took, Mother would say, "It's nice to go, and it's nice to come home."

But of all Mother's maxims, the one that stirs me most is one she likely coined herself. Each November, I think of it and recall a Thanksgiving in the mid-1920s:

It's a crisp, sunny fall afternoon. In the kitchen, Mother's basting the turkey and checking on the candied sweet potatoes and parsnips, while whole onions simmer in cream sauce at the back of the woodstove. Meanwhile, a huge kettle of boiled and drained Irish potatoes awaits my father's heavy pounding with the potato masher.

Next, Mother eases individual servings of cranberry nut Jell-O out of their molds and places them on lettuce-lined plates. After that, she mixes flour into the turkey drippings, stirring the gravy constantly to prevent lumps.

Finally, Dad calls us in. It's time to clean ourselves up and change clothes. Soon, the guests arrive—cousins, aunts, uncles and friends. And then dinner is served!

Sitting down at the laden table, we "ooh and aah" at the sight. We're ravenous. Still, we wait for Mother.

Emerging from the kitchen, she unties her apron strings. Then, with her ever-present smile, Mother takes her place at the table and Dad begins carving the turkey.

We all help ourselves from the serving dishes and then wait for the signal to begin.

Mother takes her fork, then, lifting the first bite, she cheerfully utters these memorable words, "Now, let's all just take our time."

Dear Mother, for almost three-quarters of a century, your words have endured and become a family legend. Today, any time we gather for a sit-down dinner, one voice or sometimes even a chorus of voices, is sure to repeat those words.

MAXIM MAVEN. Posing with their ever-wise mother, Emma, in the photo above, left, are Enid Maringer (right) and her brother, Frederic.

come and get it!

IS IT TURKEY YET? "Our family moved to California in the spring of 1948, and for the next few years, things were rather tough," recalls Gordon Kellen of Fontana. "But by Thanksgiving 1953, things had become a bit better and, for the first time ever, our 3-year-old daughter, Susan, saw a cooked turkey. She could hardly wait for the feast, which we all enjoyed."

EAGER EATERS. "In this shot, Janet and Craig Hutchens, my niece and nephew, were ready to sit down to Thanksgiving dinner at their Aunt Bea's house in Renton, Washington," says Beatrice Bard of Enumclaw. Check out those 1960s drapes and that knotty pine kitchen paneling.

FEAST ON FILM. This 1953 scene is from Larry Miller of Muncie, Indiana. "Every Thanksgiving, three generations gathered at my folks' house in Summitville," he says, "and a group photo was a 'must'. My sister Judy is in the center, our mother, Anna, is third from left, and cousin Kathryn is third from right. I'm the handsome young man in back!"

proud pumpkin poem

"A little poem dances through my head every year at Thanksgiving," says Evelyn Poggi of Harrington, Delaware. "I learned it when I was 6 while attending school in Staten Island."

Oh, a lone pumpkin grew on a green
pumpkin vine.
He was round, he was fat, he was yellow.
No silly jack-o'-lantern shall I make, he said
I'm determined that I'll be a useful fellow.

For the glory of the jack-o'-lantern is the candle
From the gatepost where he grins it up so high,
And the glory of the turkey is the drumstick.
But the glory of the pumpkin is the pie.

So he raised his head as the cook came around,
and he chose him at once as a winner.
His fondest wish came true—he was
a proud pumpkin pie,
And the glory of a big Thanksgiving dinner.

OUR FAVORITE GRACE

"My stepfather, Jake, always has a beautiful blessing to say before each meal, including this Irish prayer," says Sheila Hansen of Bonners Ferry, Idaho.

May God grant you always a sunbeam to warm you, a moonbeam to charm you, a sheltering angel so nothing can harm you, laughter to cheer you, faithful friends near you and, wherever you pray, Heavenly Father, to hear you.

celebrating throughout the year

CAKE HAD ADMIRERS. "Our children (from left), Mary Jacqueline, Judy and Don Jr., were gazing upon a heart-shaped cake that I had just baked for Valentine's Day, in 1965," recalls Shirley Bardella of Willcox, Arizona.

Shamrock Society

My grandmother, Susie Kelly, worked at Western Union for 20 years. That's her standing fourth from left. She was 19 when this photo was taken at the 1921 Western Union St. Patrick's Day banquet at La Plaza Hotel in Tampa, Florida.

She liked working at Western Union and even supervised four brothers and three sisters when they came to work there. She worked in the bookkeeping department.

Grandmother told me she was a "flapper" in her younger days and did the Charleston. I have so many good memories of her. She truly was like a mother to me.

—*Mike Couper, Largo, Florida*

These Flapjacks Had Fiber

My mother had a great sense of humor but was not the one to pull a practical joke—or so I thought as I sat down to breakfast on April 1, 1934.

My mouth was watering as I tackled the stack of pancakes she'd set before me. I buttered them, poured on an ample amount of syrup and cut into the stack. That was as far as I got.

No matter how hard I tried, I couldn't cut those pancakes. Something was wrong.

As I investigated the situation, I heard my mother softly say, "April fool." Then I removed the thin pieces of cardboard from the center of the top pancake.

—*Floyd Streeper, Gulfport, Mississippi*

Moms Banned from Kitchen

For years our family had been getting together at a restaurant on Mother's Day. One day the young men decided we should just celebrate at home.

Now our fabulous "Brunch Boys" serve a sumptuous buffet at our house for more than 30 family members. They do the cooking and cleanup, while we moms just come, eat and enjoy!

Being big eaters, the guys serve a typically "male" menu like scrambled eggs with cheese, bacon, sausage, biscuits and gravy, fresh fruit and possibly a dessert.

I don't know who gets a bigger kick out of this—the fellas or the mothers.

—*Carol Ritchey, Crown Point, Indiana*

> Home is where you don't have to make reservations in advance.

PATRIOTIC PICNIC. "This 1945 picture, taken in Lakewood, Ohio, shows the annual Fourth of July picnic held by my grandfather Fred Mues," notes Janis Burkhardt of North Olmsted. Such wartime Independence Days had special meaning for America. WWII was over in Europe, but fighting in the Pacific would drag on until mid-August.

1950

1953

'eggs-citing' easter tales

Springtime gatherings led to heartwarming moments.

HAVING HER CAKE. "In this 1953 slide taken in our Harrington, Washington, home, it looks like I'm ready to dive into the Easter cake, but someone stopped me," says Valerie Timm Adams of Spokane, Washington. "I think my grandmother made the cake. She was always baking creative things."

PICNIC IN THE PASTURE. "It looks like the weather was nice on Easter 1920 in Waco, Texas, when my aunt and cousins had a picnic with friends," notes Ray Sager from Houston, Texas. "Aunt Lula Prickette is holding her son Gerald. Sons Eugene and Bernard are on the right and daughter Maybelle is on the left, with her hand in front of her mouth."

yuletide traditions

Breaking Off Pieces for Peace

Before the main meal on Christmas Eve, our Polish tradition was to say grace and then pass the sacred *Oplatki*, thin wafers impressed with Nativity designs.

Dad broke off a piece and then passed his wafer to Mom, wishing her peace, love, health and happiness for the coming year. Mom did the same thing, followed by each member of the family, oldest to youngest, breaking off a piece and sending the wish.

This is my family on Christmas Eve 1946. I am the younger son, on the left.

—Stephen Lukasik
Dupont, Pennsylvania

Cookie Care Packages

Like many families, we get together in late November to make Christmas cookies. But ours isn't a typical cookie-baking experience—we turn out at least 2,000 Christmas cookies in a single day!

The tradition began in 1955 with my grandmother and great-aunt. Since then, my mother, my three children and I have joined the fun. In this 2006 photo, Gabby and Scott, my 7-year-old twins, especially enjoy rolling chocolate balls in powdered sugar, and their brother, Zachary, 9, really likes sampling them!

After our work is done, we lovingly package up the treats and send them to relatives all over the United States who eagerly await their arrival.

—Lyn Evans, Iowa Falls, Iowa

Chestnuts Roasted in a Ristola

Every Christmas, we looked forward to roasted chestnuts. Dad slit each chestnut before it was put in a heavy old iron skillet called a ristola. It was a special pan with holes punctured on the bottom. I can still smell the chestnuts as they were being roasted on the old coal stove. After we enjoyed this annual treat, the ristola was hung on the cellar rafters to await the following Christmas.

—Frances Faieta, Oceanside, California

an epiphany cake
for her crowd

Tasty treat made the Christmas season linger in their home.

By JoAnn Cooke, Reseda, California

When my kids were growing up in the 1960s and '70s in Reseda, California, we didn't rush the holiday season.

Each January 6, I baked a special cake to celebrate the feast of the Epiphany, also called Twelfth Night. I decorated a yellow cake with white frosting, and on top were a crown and candy "jewels," since the cake commemorated the visit of the wise men to the town of Bethlehem to see Jesus, the newborn King.

Because the wise men brought gold, frankincense and myrrh to the Baby Jesus, I wrapped tiny gifts, or treasures, in aluminum foil and put them in the cake batter.

Each surprise meant something special. Whoever found a dried bean would be the king of the evening. A dried pea meant that one was the queen. A penny meant the child was destined to be poor, while finding a dime ensured great wealth.

A button meant the person would be a tailor or seamstress, and a raisin signified he or she was sweet. If there was nothing in that piece of cake, then certainly God loved you.

Since I had eight children, I usually put in extra raisins and pennies and, occasionally, extra dimes and buttons. But there could be only one king and queen.

The children couldn't wait to see what treasure would be found. They'd cut up their pieces of cake to find the surprises, then unwrap them with a groan or a joyous shriek and a lot of laughter. Finally, they'd eat the crumbled cake. They still talk about the Epiphany cake today.

TASTE-TESTERS. All eight of the Cooke family children and their father, Jack, had to be wary when they were biting into Mom's Epiphany cake. Pictured (from left) are Ted, 18; Kathy, 16; Connie, 15; Mary, 14; Pat, 11; Mike, 9; Debbie, 7; and Gina, 4.

"Here they come, Mom! And Jim won't need the wish-bone—they've <u>got</u> their PLYMOUTH!"

1947

christmas 1944 served up a double helping of joy

Unplanned stop touched soldier's heart.

By T.D. Burns, Matthews, North Carolina

Before shipping out to the Japanese-held islands in the South Pacific in December 1944, we were granted liberty for December 24 and 25. I decided to try to make it home for Christmas to Wadesboro, North Carolina, from the Navy yard in Charleston, South Carolina.

In those days, hitchhiking while wearing a uniform was easy. I'd no sooner get out of one car when another would pick me up. Most of the drivers went farther than they planned just to get me closer to home. I arrived in Wadesboro by mid-afternoon.

Two of my older brothers were away, also serving in the Navy, so only my mother and sisters were living at home. They were surprised and happy to see me.

The wonderful fragrance of fresh-cut cedar from the small Christmas tree filled the air as I walked into the house. The tree was decorated with garlands, lights and all the familiar ornaments. Carols from the radio made the setting complete and much like the Christmases of my past.

Of course, Mom made a delicious supper. She had saved some of her rationed sugar for a couple of cakes, and there was a bowl of fruit and some peppermint sticks and other candy.

I didn't want this Christmas to end, but in the blink of an eye, it was morning and my mother and sister were walking me to the train station. I waved through the window as the train pulled away, and I could see tears streaming down my mother's face.

The train clicked along through farmland and pine forests as I got farther away from home. Around noon the train stopped, but there was no sign of a station. The conductor came through the car and announced there would be a 45-minute layover.

A few minutes later, the conductor came back through the car, touched me on the shoulder and whispered, "Young fellow, come with me." I followed him off the train, and I saw the engineer and the rest of the crew walking down to join us. We headed along a path through a stand of towering pines and up to a farmhouse in a clearing. This was where the train crew usually stopped for dinner, and they had invited me to join them.

What a wonderful Christmas gift, and what a dinner it was, with turkey, corn bread stuffing, ham, biscuits, vegetables and my favorite coconut cake.

Many Christmases have come and gone since then. But I will always remember 1944, when I was treated with kindness and caring by a train crew and farm family.

southern dishes flavored the season

She stirs up memories when she prepares family recipes.

By Victoria Holt Abramson, Valencia, California

Our pink old-brick home located in Hopewell, Virginia, was a sight to behold at Christmastime.

Each of the three doors sported a festive wreath of greenery and a large red bow. The front door was accented by a bright floodlight.

At night, each window held a single clear white candle, which on three levels, including the garage, made a grand total of 21 glowing lights. How proud I was as a little girl, in the early 1960s, to live in such a beautiful home.

Santa was rather predictable with the assortment of goodies he tucked inside our stockings. There were juicy and tart tangerines and nuts still in their shells—Brazil nuts, pecans and walnuts.

One time, however, I received a six-pack of Luden's cough drops; I loved them so. And once there was an array of $1 bills pinned to the outside of the stocking.

I also received a few switches in my stocking one year to remind me of my misdeeds. How can a child ever forget that?

Christmas dinner was lovingly prepared by my mother and her sister Edna. Our table held plenty of salty Smithfield ham and roast turkey as well as fluffy creamed potatoes and Southern greens.

Aunt Edna brought the oyster dressing, and my mother made her tasty corn bread dressing. There were spiced peaches, stuffed celery with pimiento cheese and cranberry sauce.

The dessert was usually homemade coconut cake, using fresh coconut my father had meticulously grated by hand. Candies had been prepared several days before—creamy brown sugar sea foam and rich chocolate nut fudge.

The recipes are mine now, and it brings me such pleasure to resurrect some of the tastes each year for my own family.

A VIRGINIA CHRISTMAS. For Victoria Holt Abramson, Christmas included good food, a lovely decorated house and a glittering tree in the basement recreation room.

santa and his helpers

When it comes to making Christmas cookies,
Mom needs little elves to assist her.
In this 1954 photo, Susan and Danny Schopp are decorating
cookies in the kitchen of their family's Madison, Wisconsin, home.
"Danny is sprinkling a paintbrush, which he used to decorate
the cookies," says Mom Kay, now of Tucson, Arizona.
Those were the days when butter, lard, salt, calories
and fat weren't things one worried about.

CHAPTER EIGHT

Unforgettable Comfort Foods

Ice cream…tomato soup…sardines? No matter what our favorite foods from the past may be, they hold a special place in our hearts simply for the comfort they brought us.

"Back in the '40s, Dad would stay up late on weekends until Mom went upstairs to bed," says Dayne Shaw of Germantown, Ohio. "Then he'd go to the kitchen to eat his beloved sardines on crackers.

"My brother and I would sneak downstairs to share the snack and quality time with our father. We sure did like sitting up late with him.

"Other quality times with Dad usually involved fishing, and we always took sardines along. (If we didn't catch anything, we'd still have fish for lunch!)

"Even today when my brother and I get together, we usually indulge in a can of sardines. Along with that pungent aroma when we open the can, all those memories of time with Dad come pouring out."

Unlock your own memories as you read sweet and savory stories from others…

secret of mama's snow cake

By Jim Luker
Chesapeake, Virginia

Daddy's voice called from downstairs, ringing as clear as sleigh bells: "God's shakin' the dandruff outta his hair!"

An excited 5-year-old, I jumped out of bed and raced across the cold floor to the frosted window. It snowed last night!

In 1938, my second-floor bedroom was on the uphill side of our Lawrenceburg, Tennessee, home. The snow had drifted so high, it seemed I could almost touch it if I opened the window.

"You know what we do today," Mother said, setting the breakfast table with smoked ham, fresh biscuits, oatmeal and honey. Yes…I knew as soon as I sat down and spotted the brown fuzzy ball Mama had placed in the center of the table.

Daddy called it a "monkey face" because it reminded him of the trained street monkeys he'd seen in France during the war. Mama laughed, then told me coconuts grew on a tree in a country where it was always warm—in a place that was never blessed with snow.

"You mean cursed," muttered Daddy. For a farmer who grew sugarcane, cotton, corn and tobacco, snow and winter were not always "blessed" times.

Now the Fun Began

Once the table was cleared, Mama took a hammer and nail and drove three holes into the "head." The fuzzy face was then balanced on top of a mason jar to let the milk drain. Next she cracked open the head with a hammer and scraped out the bright white interior.

It was my job to grate the pieces of the fragmented monkey head into a large blue-edged bowl. This made the "snowflakes" that would cover Mama's famous Snow Cake. I was careful of the grater's sharp edges. "If you skin your knuckles," Mama warned, "we'll have to throw it all out and start over." It took a long time, but I didn't mind.

CRAVED CAKE.
When the author (far right at age 5) got to help his mother (at right, with her brother), he was in coconut heaven.

I never could see Mama work her magic. It seemed like she was always hidden by the cloud of flour she created mixing the ingredients. But when the cake pans were in the oven of the wood-burning stove and my mound of snowflakes had passed inspection, I got to help Mama collect the secret ingredient.

We went to the front porch, where she scooped away the top layer of snow, then gave me a spoon to fill my cup with the fresh, feathery "ingredient."

"Some people use water in the icing," Mama explained. "But fresh snow's better."

"Did your mama show you how to make a cake?" I asked.

"My mama, and her mama before," she said.

"Will you show me?"

"When you get bigger," Mama promised. But the next year brought change. We moved to South Carolina, a place not "blessed" with snow. As the years passed, I learned to tolerate store-bought cake, for none reminded me of Mama's Snow Cake.

Then, on December 12, 1958, the day before my wedding, I awoke to whiteness. A freak weather change had brought snow. I looked out the frosted window, as I had years ago. The world was silent…then the telephone rang, sounding like so many sleigh bells.

"Yes," I answered, even before the voice came. She was only across town, but it was a voice ever inside me, one from across the years, saying, "You know what we do today."

OUR FAVORITE GRACE

"We use this grace every night before dinner,"
says Tara Puleo of Henniker, New Hampshire.
"Our two children learned it in kindergarten."

Thank You for the food before us.
Thank You for the friends beside us.
Thank You for the love between us.
Thank You, God, for everything.

nothing was better than baked goods

> If I had my life to live over, I'd live it over a bakery.

DOUGH NUT. "My grandma (with me in the photo below) lived in a little house in back of ours when I was growing up in the 1930s in San Diego, California," says Jean Beam of Knoxville, Tennessee.

"As I walked home from school, I loved nothing better than to smell the delicious aroma of homemade bread or doughnuts wafting up the street from her house. On those days, Grandma had something else special for me—she saved the doughnut holes for me to cook. On bread day, she saved dough scraps for me to play with. I still have the old doughnut cutter and the stick she used to turn the doughnuts in the oil."

CUTE AS PIE. "Grandmother was a wonderful cook, and it became tradition that I was given a bite of the crust each time a pie was baked and cooled," says Ruth Mead Davis of Milford, Ohio.

"In this 1928 photo (above), my Aunt Ruth had sneaked the pie outside for my clandestine bite at my grandparents' summer cottage on Magician Lake in Dowagiac, Michigan."

1939

'mama...I'm sick!'

Mom knew what foods made us feel better.

Tomato Soup with Saltines

When I was a little girl, if I woke up with a sore throat or tummy ache, I'd get to go lie down in Mama's bed. Within a couple of hours, Mama would have ready a bowl of cherry Jell-O. "Good for the tummy," she would say.

The next order of the day would be diluted tomato soup with a few saltine crackers on the side. Mama blew on a hot spoonful until it was "just right" before spoon-feeding it to me. Then she'd punch a hole in the top of an orange so I could suck out the sweet juice.

After a nap, I'd spend the next few hours sipping soda pop and listening to the latest popular hits on the radio. Mama would read stories to me and sometimes surprise me with a new coloring book she'd been saving.

One day of pampering was like a miracle tonic. There'll never be anybody like Mama. Without her around, it's hardly worth getting sick anymore.

—*Doris Allen, Harlingen, Texas*

Milk Shakes Soothed

In 1939, when I was 12 years old and living in Coeur d'Alene, Idaho, my oldest brother and I came down with scarlet fever. We were moved downstairs to cots in the living room, and the shades were pulled so light would not harm our eyes.

Since we couldn't read or play games, our mother took the time and effort to make us different types of milk shakes each afternoon.

She didn't have an electric beater or mixer, so milk shakes were made with milk, ice cream, fruit and syrup of various flavors, then mixed with a hand-held eggbeater. My brother and I both felt pampered.

—*Keith Yates, Tigard, Oregon*

A Treat of Stovetop Taters

If any of Mama's 14 kids got sick in the 1920s, she cooked sliced potatoes on top of a woodstove.

After the potatoes were brown on both sides, she put salt and homemade butter on them. We kids thought that made up for not feeling well.

—*Jennie Bea Gray, Street, Maryland*

new products changed what went on

the family table

Favorite Foursome

...for a wholesome beginning

Gerber's BABY FOODS

SLICED IT'S SLO-BAKED WONDER-Cut BREAD
CONTINENTAL BAKING COMPANY

COURTESY OF WONDER BREAD

GENERAL MILLS MARKETING, INC.

1920s

"Ho, ho, ho!" The **Jolly Green Giant** first appeared in advertising for the Minnesota Valley Canning Company in 1928. He was such a hit, the company was renamed for him! Eating veggies seemed a lot more fun when they came from a package featuring this colorful character.

Wonder Bread grew in popularity in 1925, when it became America's first sliced bread. During World War II, metal was conserved for the war effort and slicing blades weren't available. So the loaf with the red, blue and yellow balloons on the package again became—briefly—unsliced!

When Daniel and Dorothy Gerber began straining solid foods at home to feed their infant daughter, Sally, in 1927, **Gerber Baby Food** was born. In 1928, the company sold carrots, peas, prunes, spinach and beef vegetable soup...and debuted the famous sketch of the Gerber Baby.

1930s

Clarence Birdseye made **frozen foods** possible on a commercial scale when he developed a flash-freezing process, ensuring optimum food safety, texture and taste. In 1930, stores began carrying refrigerated cases filled with his frozen vegetables, fruits, meat, fish and oysters.

"A meal for 4…in 9 minutes." That slogan appeared on yellow boxes of **Kraft Macaroni & Cheese Dinner**, which first hit supermarkets in 1937. The 19¢ meal proved popular during the economic hardships of the Great Depression. The blue-colored box? It didn't appear until 1954.

That intriguing blend of ham and pork, **SPAM** made the scene in 1937. During World War II, over 100 million pounds of the "miracle meat in a can" were shipped overseas to feed allied troops…and plenty of folks enjoyed it on the home front, too.

1940s

Earl Tupper used polyethylene, a new plastic created in 1942, to develop an airtight covered bowl with a "burping" seal. **Tupperware** was originally sold in retail stores but soon became available only through home "Tupperware parties." Millions of party invitations followed.

Love those O's! General Mills introduced Cheerioats, the first ready-to-eat oat cereal, in 1941. In a bright yellow box with a big blue circle, Cheerioats also had a mascot—Cheeri O' Leary. The cereal's name was shortened to **Cheerios** in 1945.

The first **microwave ovens** appeared in 1947, but they weren't exactly practical for home use. These primitive versions stood 5½ feet tall, weighed 750 pounds and cost $5,000! Countertop models arrived in the 1960s, and by the mid-1970s, more of them were being sold than gas ranges.

A dessert shortcut gained widespread popularity when General Mills offered **Betty Crocker cake mixes** in 1948. Home cooks who were tired of baking from scratch now had an alternative that still tasted good. In other words, they could have their cake and eat it, too!

BETTMANN/CORBIS

PINNACLE FOODS GROUP LLC

KRAFTFOODS.COM

GENERAL MILLS MARKETING, INC.

GENERAL MILLS MARKETING, INC.

TUPPERWARE BRANDS CORPORATION

WILLIAM GOTTLIEB/CORBIS

What was the best thing before sliced bread?

1950s

With *I Love Lucy* and other hit TV shows, it's no wonder Americans were glued to the tube in the 1950s. Swanson made it easy to stay there when the company debuted **TV dinners** in 1953. For 98¢, TV watchers could enjoy a main course and several side dishes—all on a disposable, oven-ready tray.

The collapsible, easy-to-store stands known as **TV trays** were marketed nationally in 1952—before Swanson started the TV dinner craze. Those dinners created a permanent spot for TV trays in homes across America…and led to increasingly dusty dining room tables.

By the time the 1950s rolled around, sugary soft drinks had existed for decades. But weight-conscious folks cheered when **Diet Rite Cola**, the first zero-calorie diet soda offered nationally, appeared in 1958. By the early 1960s, it was the fourth most popular soda in the United States.

1960s

A milkman delivering glass bottles of milk…it was part of everyday life for most Americans until the middle of the twentieth century. In the 1950s, paper cartons began replacing many bottles, and the **plastic milk container** was introduced commercially in 1964.

Who can resist the lovable giggle and belly poke of Poppin' Fresh? The **Pillsbury Doughboy** first won hearts in a TV commercial for Crescent Rolls in 1965. Since that time, the cute character has been in hundreds of commercials featuring more than 50 Pillsbury products.

In 1966, sweet tooths could top off their desserts in a jiffy thanks to **Cool Whip**. The ready-made, frozen whipped topping quickly replaced real whipped cream for many home cooks and became a holiday staple.

cold snow cones on a hot summer day

Imagine having this much fun for a nickel.

By Earlene Massie, San Antonio, Texas

The uphill path that ran from the 300 block of Browning Street in Pampa, Texas, to a tiny white stand was hot. The melting tar clung to the bottom of our bare feet and oozed between our toes.

From time to time, we came upon a patch of weeds and stopped to cool our feet before continuing our mission. We had a goal in mind, and not even hot tar could deter us.

Grasped in each of our sweaty hands was a nickel. The wooden stand could be seen from the moment we entered the pathway, and we kept it in our sights as we thought about what flavor we would order.

Even before arriving, we would hear the whirring of the machine as the man fed the ice into the crusher. That made us walk even quicker.

Within three or four minutes, our destination was reached. The snow cone stand cast a cooling shadow that made it bearable to stand in front of the window as we contemplated our flavor preference.

Taking the metal ladle, the woman piled the finely crushed ice into the white paper cone, making sure to round the top. She made the rainbow cones appear as art as she pushed the plunger on one flavor and then another.

I could never figure as to why the coconut flavor was blue. But who cared? It was delicious!

Coconut, strawberry, lemon, orange, grape, lime, rainbow—it was difficult to choose.

Never knowing when we might be the fortunate recipients of another nickel, we wanted to make this one count. We didn't want any regrets in our decision.

Just as expected, the ice was thirst-quenching and the sweet juice delicious! We dawdled on our journey down the path, as we didn't want to spill a single drop.

We traded sips, trying to decide which flavor we would choose on our next trip and declaring who had chosen best that day.

Before we could consume it all, the juice began to trickle out the wet thinning bottom of the paper cone and make designs as it ran down our arms. We sucked on the bottom of the cup so as not to waste a delicious drop.

Soon it was gone, and our tongues, hands, arms, legs and feet were stained with the color of the refreshing memorable treat.

As we crossed the street to the small apartment complex to resume our play, we wondered when we could get our hands on another nickel.

refreshing summer treats are frozen in time

From ice cream to snow cones, cool snacks put us in good humor.

Hot for Snow Cones

Saturdays were beach days during my 1948 summer in Texas. I'd grab a couple of hot buttered tortillas on my way out the door to the beach, then start collecting pop bottles. My goal was 20 bottles for 20 cents, enough to buy two of the most scrumptious snow cones.

There were just two flavors…Hawaiian punch and sugar milk. The vendor made these to order, shaving ice from a huge block wrapped in a gunnysack. For cups, he used jelly glasses, which he washed and reused.

—*Rafael Villalobos, Aransas Pass, Texas*

Bell-Ringing Dessert

In the early '20s, when I was about 6 years old, I remember sitting on the front porch after supper, listening for the bell announcing the ice cream wagon. I could hear it from a block away, enough time for us to "get ready."

If Dad was in a good mood, he'd reach into his pocket for a quarter and tell me, "Go get the dish!" He meant the favorite china bowl, which the ice cream man filled to the top with homemade vanilla ice cream. There were no other flavors.

Back on the porch, Mother had the dessert dishes ready. What delicious memories!

—*Mary Becker, Boynton Beach, Florida*

Ice Cream Icebreaker

My dad was in the Air Force back in the '50s, so our family moved frequently from base to base. My mother carried with us a surefire way to make new friends in the neighborhood wherever we were.

She'd bring the ice cream maker out onto the front porch and invite the neighbors to join us for an ice cream social.

—*Rick McNelly, Belvidere, Illinois*

TWO FOR ONE. "I took this picture in August 1953 of my nieces, Julie and Frances Miller, sharing an ice cream cone in a neighborhood park in Dayton, Ohio," recalls Richard Miller of Kettering. "The girls are now married and still have a sisterly relationship, even if they don't share licks on the same cone."

hand-cranked ice cream made the day

By Karla Kincaid, Hamilton, Ohio

I grew up next door to my Grandma Rooke, and we always had a great summer picnic when Grandma's brother, Uncle Jess, came to visit us from Norfolk, Virginia.

There was corn on the cob, green beans, mounds of mashed potatoes, sliced fresh tomatoes, fried chicken, plus apple and cherry pies, and a rich chocolate cake topped with a delicious brown-sugar frosting.

But the highlight of the day was when Dad retrieved the green wooden bucket from Grandma's basement. Time to crank the ice cream!

A golden mixture had been prepared earlier and poured into the shiny metal canister, the beaters inserted and the lid placed on top. The canister was placed inside the bucket and crushed ice was poured around the canister and salt was added.

A heavy metal crank was fastened on top, and the work began. All of us kids took turns cranking while the ice cream was soft. Our arms would ache, and we'd just pass the job off to a brother, sister or cousin.

As the milky mixture would begin to become ice cream, turning that handle got harder, and the kids, one by one, returned to their games.

I was the last child to leave the cranking. I just liked being with my dad a little longer. After a while, he always sent me to play and then finished the cranking.

Then he removed the crank and lid from the canister, being careful not to get salt in the ice cream. The beaters were placed in a large bowl and—as I later learned—Dad partook of his reward. He licked the beaters!

> *The highlight of the day was when Dad retrieved the green wooden bucket from Grandma's basement. Time to crank the ice cream!*

The cold metal lid was returned to the canister, and a small brown cork covered the hole. Fresh, clean ice was piled on and an empty brown ice bag covered it all.

We were told it had to sit under the ice for 1 hour, though I'm sure it never did.

As the frozen gold was uncovered, we all gathered around with bowls and spoons in hand.

Even today, this treat is sure to brighten my spirits.

can't beat cold root beer

By Audrey Casperson, McKeesport, Pennsylvania

When one scorcher turned into another in the dog days of summer near McKeesport, Pennsylvania, Pap would roll his eyes toward the bright sun and say, "Boy, an ice-cold root beer would sure taste good."

In the early '30s, making root beer in Weldon Cabin Sites where we lived was a respected art. If you were the first to set out a batch, your standing in the cabins went up a few notches.

When we made root beer, it was my job to gather the old amber beer bottles from under the cabin and to wash them in hot soapy water. As they sparkled in the sun, Pap made the brew.

He filled an old enamel dishpan with water and heated it to lukewarm. Next he added sugar, dry yeast and the root beer syrup. When it had dissolved into an amber nectar, he filled the bottles with a dipper and funnel, leaving 2 inches of air space at the top.

He then sat the bottle on the small platform of the bottle capper, applied a crown cap to the lip and pressed down with the capper jack. Carefully, we carried each bottle to a grassy spot behind the cabin where the sun beat down.

In a few days, we saw bubbles form on the inside of the bottles. About the fifth day, Pap did a quality check. It was a momentous occasion. The cabin kids would fidget around the grassy spot, each with an old jelly jar or a clean soup can, anticipating a taste.

Pap picked up a bottle, carefully wiping off any clinging grass with his red handkerchief. Then he slowly pried off the cap and listened for the fizz.

The foaming nectar would bubble up over the top and cascade down the sides as we kids cheered and tried to catch the fizz in our jars.

We knew we were in for a special treat. After the bottles chilled for a few hours in a bucket of ice, we could truly say, "Boy, an ice-cold drink of root beer sure tastes good."

popcorn was a satisfying snack

When I was growing up in the '50s, we didn't have the extra money to buy all the snacks that kids eat today. For our family, the best treat was popcorn. My sister Sandy (left) would fill the pan full of kernels, and we kids could hardly wait till it started popping. The popcorn tasted best if we could eat it while we watched Dad's home movies on the wall in the living room.

—*Donna Deem*
Fort Mill, South Carolina

"Fresh up" with Seven-Up!

Copyright 1953, The Seven-Up Company

The All-Family Drink
You like it... it likes you!

Here's a "plot" for happy autumn evenings... the fire glowing on the hearth, the corn a-popping, and plenty of sparkling, crystal-clear 7-Up! This lively favorite is so pure, so good, so wholesome that young folks, old folks, folks of *all* ages may "fresh up" to their hearts' content.

Get a family supply of 24 bottles. *Buy 7-Up by the case. Or get the handy 7-Up Family Pack. Easy-lift center handle... easy to store.*
Buy 7-Up wherever you see those bright 7-Up signs

1953

preserving the season's finest produce

Canned goods filled cellars and fed families for months.

By June Titus, Lincoln, Nebraska

When I was a child, we always had a vegetable garden. As the tiny cucumbers started forming on the vines, we kept a daily check. The first picking of a peck basket had Mother bringing out her special pans and crocks. When I left for school, she was busy scrubbing cucumbers and putting them down in water with pickling salt.

As the days went by, Mother's nine-day pickles went through their stages of preparation. I knew when the first waft of vinegar greeted me at the door that the pickles were at stage three. Stage four added spices to the delightful aroma.

Then, at last, they were packed in jars, sealed and carried downstairs to the waiting shelves. The best time lay ahead—the winter day when a jar was opened and we finally bit into a crisp, delicious pickle.

A vegetable garden was at the top of our list of things to do when my husband and I bought our first house. Leaning on our childhood experiences of helping with gardening, we were rewarded with a good crop of cucumbers. Mom's nine-day pickle recipe came out of my recipe box, and I carefully followed her directions. When I reached steps three and four, I took deep sniffs of satisfaction.

My kitchen smelled just like Mother's.

We pray in microwave time, but the answer usually comes slow-cooked.

JUST PEACHY.
"My husband was a merchandiser for the American Fruit Growers," says Rose Cunningham from Decatur, Illinois. "During peach season, he brought home three crates of peaches for me to can. What delicious flavor they had! We lived in Waterloo, Iowa, when this photo of me was taken."

last lick

"Mother had just finished filling up the jars with homemade jelly when this photograph was snapped in 1928," shares Ruth Fanger of Monroe, Oregon. "My brother, Lee, and I are enjoying every little taste left in the pan on the steps of our farmhouse near Coquille, Oregon."

Unforgettable Comfort Foods

homemade dishes celebrated our heritage

Friends and family enjoyed ethnic specialties throughout the year.

Cookies Put Spring in Her Step

Every Christmas, Grandma made *springerle*, a German cookie, and let me help her make the imprint in the dough. It had to set overnight and was baked in the morning. Oh, to wake up to that aroma! When Grandma sent me to school with warm *springerle* to eat on the way, I felt like the richest kid in the world!

—*Ruth Smalley, Roselle, New Jersey*

Lucky Treat from Romania

My parents were from Romania, and each New Year's Day, Mother made a dessert called *plachenta*.

She'd cover the table with a cloth, place a ball of raised dough in the center and pull on it until tissue-thin. Then a filling was sprinkled over the dough, either spinach and cottage cheese, poppy seed, nuts, or apples with spices.

When rolled up, it was about 2 inches in diameter and 4 feet long. Mother would wash a dime, wrap it in foil and hide it in the dough before baking. Whoever found the coin would have good luck all year.

—*Nicholas Yorga, Cibolo, Texas*

OUR FAVORITE GRACE

"As a child, I learned this grace at summer Bible camp and taught it to our children when they were young," recalls Elaine Turner of Frederick, Maryland.

Come, Lord Jesus, be our guest,
our morning joy, our evening rest.
And with our daily bread impart,
Thy love and peace to every heart.

mama's christmas ravioli

By Dorothy Ciminelli Delmonte, Buffalo, New York

For as long as I can remember, each Christmas I awoke to the fragrance of Mama's tomato sauce cooking on the stove.

Daddy had died when I was 5, in 1949, leaving Mama to raise five children. Still, she was determined that my brothers and I would grow up knowing the traditions our grandparents had brought from Italy.

On Christmas Eve, we put up our tree and set out the manger scene, including a rustic handmade creche, and we opened presents Christmas morning.

The kitchen in our farmhouse near Buffalo didn't have an ample counter, so Mama set up the ironing board on holidays. Then she'd place the tiny pale yellow pillows of ravioli in rows on the board.

With a sheet of dough rolled flat before her, Mama dropped fluffy white mounds of ricotta in straight lines. Then she'd fold the dough over the ricotta, cutting out squares.

It was my job to press the corners of the tiny pillows, sealing the ricotta inside, but my clumsy hands were never as skillful as Mama's. Eventually she'd assign me the task of setting the dining room table.

We might have 20 or 30 people for the meal, including children seated at card tables in the living room.

Looking back, I realize what a hardship this feast must have been for her.

When Mama died, we held a sale and someone bought the ironing board. I couldn't keep back the tears, and I'm certain that the stranger who bought it wondered why on earth anyone would cry over an ironing board.

All I could see was Mama…and those neat little rows of ravioli.

fresh eggs and
fried chicken

Raising chickens was delicious fun for the whole family.

By Bonnie Crace Harrison, McDermott, Ohio

Seeking a better place to raise my siblings and me, my parents, John and Blanche Crace, moved us from Oak Hill, Ohio, to a rented cottage near Jackson in 1939.

There was a barn, some outbuildings, a pond and acreage for a garden. I was 10 years old, and my five younger siblings and I thrived in our new environment.

One of Mother's pleasures was raising chickens. Each spring, she'd buy about 100 chicks—half, white leghorns for eggs and the other half, white rocks for eating.

We children looked forward to the arrival of the adorable cheeping balls of yellow fluff and helped prepare a place to keep them warm until they were old enough to be moved into the chicken house.

The laying hens kept our family of eight supplied with eggs, and if there was an excess, Mom had no trouble selling them.

When the fryers were large enough, we added them to our menu. Mom was a wonderful cook, and her iron-skillet-fried chicken was second to none.

The few chickens that grew old and fat were stewed. Homemade dumplings were added to the broth to make one of my favorite dishes.

I remember one morning in the 1940s. It was the custom to call on relatives and friends on Sunday afternoons. If you stayed home, you were almost sure to have visitors.

After church, Mom was preparing dinner and some relatives arrived. Dad killed a couple of chickens and Mom fixed more vegetables and biscuits.

Carload after carload of relatives and friends, some from Kentucky, kept arriving. Each time, more chickens were killed and the women helped prepare the meal—all without today's modern conveniences.

Dad set up a long table on the large front lawn, and that afternoon my parents fed 32 people! Our home was one where everyone always received a warm welcome and a delicious meal.

MORE THAN CHICKEN FEED. Bonnie Crace Harrison's mom and brother Donny (left) feed the chickens on their farm near Jackson, Ohio, in 1940.

slice of life

Growing up in the '30s and '40s, I spent many happy days
at Pa Tom's house in eastern Louisa County, Virginia.
Pa Tom was my mother's father, and I have special memories
of his watermelons. He let the whole family help prepare
the watermelon patch and plant the seeds at just the right depth.
By late July, we were toting watermelons to the well house
to be placed in cold water to cool. The anticipation reached
near-anxiety stage…we could almost taste those beauties!
Soon we were diving in like the boys in the photo.

—*Lewis Mills, Topeka, Kansas*

Unforgettable Comfort Foods

CHAPTER NINE

My Moms' Best Meal

When you think back in time to your favorite moments spent at the kitchen or dining room table, enjoying one of Mom's many home-cooked meals is likely at the top of the list. There was no better way for Mom to express her feelings for the family than by taking time to prepare a mouth-watering meal seasoned with lots of love and care.

On the following pages, 10 cooks from across the country share delightful dinners that their moms served while they were growing up.

Fried Chicken with Pan Gravy, Sage Meat Loaf, Barbecued Pork Sandwiches and Caesar Orange Roughy are just a taste of the outstanding main courses you'll find that suit any day or occasion.

And don't forget everyone's favorite—dessert! A sample of the sweets includes Chocolate Ring Cake, Fresh Raspberry Pie, Iced Anise Cookies and Jubilee Sundaes.

These "kids" may be grown and cooking for their own families now, but the unforgettable foods they share here still make their mouths' water.

We think they'll make you mighty hungry, too...

raves for roast chicken

By Joann Jensen
Lowell, Indiana

I grew up in a hardworking farm family full of big appetites. When the six of us gathered at the table, the first thing we did was say grace. Other than that, we didn't talk much…unless it was to ask someone to pass the chicken!

Our only concern was whether or not Mom made enough for second helpings. And everyone wanted seconds of her wonderful meals. There never seemed to be any leftovers.

My mom, Edna Hoffman *(above right, at left)*, of Hebron, Indiana, was raised on a farm, too. I don't think she ever prepared a recipe using a boxed cake mix or heated a frozen dinner. And she's never been afraid to try something new.

Her meals weren't extravagant, but boy, were they good! Hard work, especially at harvesttime, made Mom's cooking taste even better.

While my two brothers helped our dad, Marty, with farm work, my sister and I helped Mom with canning, freezing and tending our huge garden. We both learned from Mom in the kitchen, but I also picked up many skills in 4-H and at school. Now I cook for my husband, Steve. We have two grown daughters, Jamie and Kellie.

This favorite meal of mine features Cherry Gelatin Salad, Roast Chicken with Oyster Stuffing, Potato Vegetable Medley and Chocolate Ring Cake. I hope you'll give it a try!

on the menu
Roast Chicken with Oyster Stuffing
Potato Vegetable Medley
Cherry Gelatin Salad
Chocolate Ring Cake

Roast Chicken with Oyster Stuffing

PREP: 35 MINUTES
BAKE: 2 HOURS + STANDING
YIELD: 6 SERVINGS (4 CUPS STUFFING)

- 1   can (8 ounces) whole oysters
- 1/4 cup butter, cubed
- 1   celery rib, chopped
- 1   small onion, chopped
- 2   tablespoons minced fresh parsley
- 1/2 teaspoon Italian seasoning
- 3   cups cubed bread, lightly toasted
- 1   roasting chicken (6 pounds)
- 1/4 cup butter, melted
- 1 to 2 teaspoons paprika

1. Drain the oysters, reserving the liquid; coarsely chop the oysters. Set aside. In a small skillet, melt the butter. Add the celery and onion; saute until tender. Stir in parsley and Italian seasoning. Place bread cubes in a large bowl; add the butter mixture, oysters and 1/4 cup reserved oyster liquid.

2. Just before baking, loosely stuff chicken with stuffing. Place breast side up on a rack in a roasting pan; tie drumsticks together. Combine melted butter and paprika; brush over chicken.

3. Bake, uncovered, at 350° for 2 to 2-1/2 hours or until a meat thermometer reads 180° for the chicken and 165° for the stuffing, basting occasionally with the pan drippings. (Cover loosely with foil if the chicken browns too quickly.)

4. Cover the chicken and let stand for 10 minutes before removing the stuffing and carving chicken. Skim fat and thicken pan juices if desired.

Potato Vegetable Medley

PREP: 10 MINUTES
BAKE: 40 MINUTES
YIELD: 6 SERVINGS

- 6 small red potatoes, quartered
- 16 baby carrots, halved lengthwise
- 1 small onion, cut into wedges
- 1/2 cup chicken broth
- 1 1/4 teaspoons seasoned salt, divided
- 2 medium zucchini, chopped
- 2 tablespoons minced fresh parsley

1. In a 2-qt. baking dish coated with cooking spray, combine the potatoes, carrots, onion, chicken broth and 1 teaspoon seasoned salt. Cover and bake at 400° for 30 minutes.

2. Stir in zucchini and remaining seasoned salt. Bake 10-15 minutes longer or until vegetables are tender. Sprinkle with parsley.

NUTRITION FACTS: 3/4 cup equals 59 calories, trace fat (trace saturated fat), trace cholesterol, 424 mg sodium, 13 g carbohydrate, 2 g fiber, 2 g protein. DIABETIC EXCHANGES: 1 vegetable, 1/2 starch.

Cherry Gelatin Salad

PREP: 15 MINUTES + CHILLING
YIELD: 6 SERVINGS

- 1 can (15 ounces) pitted dark sweet cherries
- 1 package (3 ounces) cherry gelatin
- 1 cup cold water
- 1 tablespoon lemon juice
- 2 medium bananas, sliced
- 1/4 cup chopped pecans
Additional sliced banana and chopped pecans, optional

1. Drain cherries, reserving liquid in a 1-cup measuring cup; add enough water to measure 1 cup. In a small saucepan, bring mixture to a boil. Remove from the heat; stir in gelatin until dissolved. Stir in cold water and lemon juice.

2. Cover and refrigerate until syrupy, about 40 minutes. Fold in bananas, pecans and cherries. Transfer to a 6-cup mold coated with cooking spray. Refrigerate until firm. Unmold onto a serving platter. Garnish with additional banana and pecans if desired.

NUTRITION FACTS: 1/2 cup equals 169 calories, 4 g fat (trace saturated fat), 0 cholesterol, 35 mg sodium, 34 g carbohydrate, 3 g fiber, 3 g protein. DIABETIC EXCHANGES: 1 starch, 1 fruit, 1 fat.

Chocolate Ring Cake

PREP: 30 MINUTES + COOLING
BAKE: 40 MINUTES + COOLING
YIELD: 12 SERVINGS

- 3 squares (1 ounce each) unsweetened chocolate, chopped
- 1/2 cup boiling water
- 1 cup shortening
- 1 3/4 cups sugar
- 4 eggs
- 2 teaspoons vanilla extract
- 2 1/4 cups all-purpose flour
- 1 1/2 teaspoons salt
- 1 teaspoon baking soda
- 1/2 teaspoon baking powder
- 1 cup buttermilk
- 1 1/2 cups black walnuts

FROSTING
- 6 tablespoons butter, cubed
- 1/3 cup milk
- 1/3 cup sugar
- 2 squares (1 ounce each) unsweetened chocolate, chopped
- 1 tablespoon light corn syrup
- 1/4 teaspoon salt
- 1 teaspoon vanilla extract

1. In a small bowl, stir chocolate and boiling water until chocolate is melted; cool for 10 minutes. In a large bowl, cream shortening and sugar until light and fluffy. Add eggs, one at a time, beating well after each addition. Stir in vanilla and chocolate mixture.

2. Combine the flour, salt, baking soda and baking powder; add to the creamed mixture alternately with buttermilk, beating well after each addition. Stir in the walnuts.

3. Pour into a greased and floured 10-in. fluted tube pan. Bake at 350° for 40-50 minutes or until a toothpick inserted near the center comes out clean. Cool for 10 minutes before removing from pan to a wire rack to cool completely.

4. For frosting, in a small saucepan, combine the butter, milk, sugar, chocolate, corn syrup and salt. Cook and stir over low heat until blended. Remove from the heat; stir in vanilla. Beat with a mixer for 15 minutes or until mixture begins to thicken. Refrigerate until frosting reaches spreading consistency. Frost top and sides of cake. Refrigerate leftovers.

RAISING AN EXTRA-BIG FAMILY DIDN'T STOP HER INEXHAUSTIBLE MOM FROM SERVING UP SCRUMPTIOUS HOMEMADE MEALS DAY AFTER DAY AND SATISFYING EVERYONE AT THE TABLE.

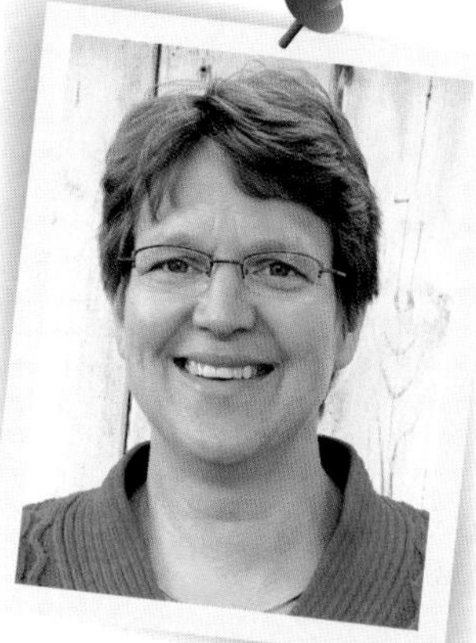

a slice of family life

By Emily Dennis
Hancock, Michigan

How my mother, Anne Heinonen *(above right)*, found time to make homemade dinners every day is beyond me. She had a full-time job raising 14 children in Howell, Michigan! Still, she made everything from scratch.

One of the things we loved when we walked in the door after school was the aroma of her Sage Meat Loaf and Seasoned Mashed Potatoes. Mom rounded out the meal with Tasty Tossed Salad and irresistible Fresh Raspberry Pie.

The best part of the meat loaf is the sweet topping. And we always got excited when we saw the big bowl of creamy mashed potatoes on the table.

It wasn't easy getting us to eat salads, but my mom made them appealing with her delicious mayonnaise dressing.

The raspberry pie was practically a staple at our house in late summer. My dad, Fred, loves this pie served with vanilla ice cream.

Whether it was Sunday dinner or a weeknight meal, we always sat down at the table together. As you can imagine, mealtime was full of chaos but also full of great conversation and lots of laughs.

These days, I look forward to visits to my parents' house. I'm a stay-at-home mom, and my husband, Matt, is a middle school teacher. We have three children—Kirsten, Cale and Brady.

Kirsten, our oldest child, already loves to help me in the kitchen. I hope she'll look back with fond memories of warm-from-the-oven cookies and home-cooked meals, just as I do.

on the menu

Sage Meat Loaf
Tasty Tossed Salad
Seasoned Mashed Potatoes
Fresh Raspberry Pie

fresh raspberry pie
RECIPE ON PAGE 173

Sage Meat Loaf

PREP: 15 MINUTES
BAKE: 65 MINUTES
YIELD: 6 SERVINGS

1 egg, beaten
2/3 cup milk
1 tablespoon Worcestershire sauce
1 cup crushed saltines
1/4 cup finely chopped onion
1 teaspoon salt
1/2 teaspoon rubbed sage
1/4 teaspoon pepper
1 1/2 pounds ground beef
1/4 cup ketchup
3 tablespoons brown sugar
1 teaspoon ground mustard
1/4 teaspoon ground nutmeg

1. In a large bowl, combine the first eight ingredients. Crumble beef over the mixture and mix well. Pat meat mixture into an ungreased 9-in. x 5-in. x 3-in. loaf pan. Bake, uncovered, at 350° for 50 minutes.

2. Combine ketchup, brown sugar, mustard and nutmeg; spread over the top. Bake 15-20 minutes longer or until meat is no longer pink and a meat thermometer reads 160°. Let meat loaf stand for 10 minutes before slicing.

Tasty Tossed Salad

PREP/TOTAL TIME: 25 MINUTES
YIELD: 6 SERVINGS

2 cups torn iceberg lettuce
1 cup fresh cauliflowerets
1 cup fresh broccoli florets
1 cup shredded carrots
1/3 cup chopped red onion
6 bacon strips, cooked and crumbled
1 cup (4 ounces) shredded cheddar cheese

DRESSING
3/4 cup mayonnaise
3 tablespoons sugar
3 tablespoons lemon juice

1. In a large salad bowl, combine the lettuce, cauliflower, broccoli, carrots, onion and bacon. Top with cheddar cheese.

2. Combine the mayonnaise, sugar and lemon juice. Pour over lettuce mixture and toss to coat. Serve immediately.

Seasoned Mashed Potatoes

PREP: 15 MINUTES
COOK: 20 MINUTES
YIELD: 6 SERVINGS

3 pounds potatoes, peeled and quartered (about 9 medium)
2 packages (3 ounces each) cream cheese, softened
6 tablespoons butter, softened
1/4 cup milk
3/4 teaspoon seasoned salt
3/4 teaspoon pepper
1/4 teaspoon onion salt

1. Place the potatoes in a large saucepan and cover with water. Bring to a boil. Reduce heat; cover and cook for 15-20 minutes or until tender. Drain.

2. In a large mixing bowl, mash potatoes. Add remaining ingredients; beat until fluffy.

Fresh Raspberry Pie

PREP: 35 MINUTES + STANDING
BAKE: 50 MINUTES + COOLING
YIELD: 6-8 SERVINGS

2 cups all-purpose flour
1 tablespoon sugar
1/2 teaspoon salt
3/4 cup shortening
1 egg, beaten
3 tablespoons cold water
1 tablespoon white vinegar

FILLING
1 1/3 cups sugar
2 tablespoons quick-cooking tapioca
2 tablespoons cornstarch
5 cups fresh or frozen unsweetened raspberries, thawed
1 tablespoon butter

TOPPING
1 tablespoon milk
1 tablespoon sugar

1. In a large bowl, combine the flour, sugar and salt; cut in shortening until the mixture resembles coarse crumbs. Combine egg, water and vinegar; stir into flour mixture just until moistened. Divide the dough in half so that one ball is slightly larger than the other; wrap each in plastic wrap. Refrigerate dough for 30 minutes or until easy to handle.

2. Meanwhile, in another large bowl, combine the sugar, tapioca, cornstarch and raspberries; let stand for 15 minutes.

3. On a lightly floured surface, roll out the larger ball of dough to fit a 9-in. pie plate. Transfer the dough to pie plate; trim even with edge. Add raspberry filling; dot with butter.

4. Roll out remaining dough to fit top of pie; place over filling. Trim, seal and flute edges. Cut slits in top. Brush with milk; sprinkle with sugar. Bake at 350° for 50-55 minutes or until crust is golden brown and filling is bubbly. Cool on a wire rack.

regal pork roast

By Christine Frazier
Auburndale, Florida

When it comes to special-occasion meals, my mom, Louise Precourt *(above right, at left)*, has been an inspiration.

While I was growing up, she relished hosting large family gatherings after church. I'll never forget them.

My mouth waters as I recall one particular dinner featuring crown roast of pork with a savory wild rice stuffing. Mom served it with Peas a la Francaise (a favorite), tender Sour Cream Yeast Rolls and yummy Jubilee Sundaes.

This impressive menu is perfect for Easter or other festive occasions. Easter has always been very special for our family, and Mom hosts the best egg hunts for her grandchildren and great-grandchildren.

Our family—Mom, Dad, my sister, three brothers and me—moved a lot because my dad was an aerospace engineer. Mom was a teacher. Now, my parents are retired and live in Winter Haven, Florida.

Mom still cooks but no longer does it all when we get together. Instead, everyone chips in...and there's always lots of laughter!

I am who I am because of my mom, and cooking is our shared passion. I am proud to say that she is both my mother and my best friend.

I'm happy to share this meal—it's one of her best! I just know you and your family will adore it, too!

on the menu
Crown Roast with Wild Rice Stuffing
Sour Cream Yeast Rolls
Peas a la Francaise
Jubilee Sundaes

Crown Roast with Wild Rice Stuffing

PREP: 15 MINUTES
BAKE: 2-3/4 HOURS + STANDING
YIELD: 15 SERVINGS (12 CUPS STUFFING)

- 1 teaspoon dried thyme
- 1 teaspoon fennel seed, crushed
- 1 teaspoon salt
- 1/2 teaspoon pepper
- 1 pork crown roast (about 9 pounds)
- 1 cup unsweetened apple juice

STUFFING
- 2 quarts water
- 2 cups uncooked wild rice
- 2 teaspoons salt, optional
- 1/2 pound sliced fresh mushrooms
- 2 medium onions, chopped
- 2 tablespoons butter
- 2 pounds seasoned bulk pork sausage

Fresh kale and pickled whole beets, optional

1. Combine the thyme, fennel, salt and pepper; sprinkle over roast. Place on a rack in a large shallow roasting pan. Cover rib ends with foil. Bake, uncovered, at 350° for 2-3/4 to 3-1/4 hours or until a meat thermometer reads 160°, basting occasionally with apple juice.

2. For stuffing, in a large saucepan, bring the water, wild rice and salt if desired to a boil. Reduce heat; cover and simmer for 45-60 minutes or until tender.

3. In a large skillet, saute the fresh mushrooms and onions in the butter until tender. Transfer to a large bowl. In the same skillet, cook the pork sausage over medium heat until no longer pink; drain. Drain the rice; add the rice and sausage to the mushroom mixture and stir until blended.

4. Transfer the roast to a serving platter; let stand for 15 minutes. Remove foil. Spoon the stuffing into center of roast. Garnish the platter with kale and beets if desired. Cut between ribs to serve.

Sour Cream Yeast Rolls

PREP: 35 MINUTES + RISING
BAKE: 25 MINUTES
YIELD: 1 DOZEN

2¹/2 to 3 cups all-purpose flour
  2 tablespoons sugar
  1 package (¹/4 ounce) active dry yeast
  1 teaspoon salt
  1 cup sour cream
¹/4 cup water
  3 tablespoons butter, divided
  1 egg

1. In a large bowl, combine 1-1/2 cups flour, sugar, yeast and salt. In a small saucepan, heat the sour cream, water and 2 tablespoons butter to 120°-130°; add to dry ingredients. Beat on medium speed for 2 minutes. Add egg and 1/2 cup flour; beat 2 minutes longer. Stir in enough remaining flour to form a soft dough.

2. Turn onto a floured surface; knead until smooth and elastic, about 6-8 minutes. Place in a greased bowl, turning once to grease the top. Cover and let rise in a warm place until doubled, about 1 hour.

3. Punch down dough. Turn onto a lightly floured surface; divide into 12 pieces. Shape each into a ball. Place in a greased 13-in. x 9-in. baking pan. Cover and let rise until doubled, about 30 minutes.

4. Bake at 375° for 25-30 minutes or until golden brown. Melt remaining butter; brush over rolls. Remove from pan to a wire rack.

Peas a la Francaise

PREP/TOTAL TIME: 30 MINUTES
YIELD: 12 SERVINGS (1/2 CUP EACH)

1¹/2 cups pearl onions
¹/4 cup butter, cubed
¹/4 cup water
  1 tablespoon sugar
  1 teaspoon salt
¹/4 teaspoon dried thyme
¹/4 teaspoon dried chervil
¹/4 teaspoon pepper
  2 packages (16 ounces each) frozen peas, thawed
  2 cups shredded lettuce

1. In a large saucepan, bring 6 cups water to a boil. Add the pearl onions; boil for 5 minutes. Drain and rinse the pearl onions in cold water; peel.

2. In the same saucepan, melt butter over medium heat. Stir in the onions, water, sugar and seasonings. Add peas and lettuce; stir until blended. Cover and cook for 6-8 minutes or until tender. Serve with a slotted spoon.

NUTRITION FACTS: 1/2 cup equals 112 calories, 4 g fat (2 g saturated fat), 10 mg cholesterol, 315 mg sodium, 15 g carbohydrate, 4 g fiber, 4 g protein. DIABETIC EXCHANGES: 1 starch, 1 fat.

Jubilee Sundaes

PREP: 10 MINUTES
COOK: 10 MINUTES + COOLING
YIELD: 2 CUPS SAUCE

1/3 cup sugar
  2 tablespoons cornstarch
1/8 teaspoon salt
  1 can (14 1/2 ounces) pitted tart cherries
  2 teaspoons lemon juice
1/4 teaspoon grated lemon peel
1/4 teaspoon almond extract
Vanilla ice cream

1. In a large saucepan, combine the sugar, cornstarch and salt. Drain cherries, reserving juice; set cherries aside. Stir cherry juice into cornstarch mixture until smooth. Bring to a boil over medium heat, stirring constantly. Cook and stir for 1-2 minutes or until thickened.

2. Remove from the heat; stir in the lemon juice and peel, extract and reserved cherries. Cool to room temperature. Serve with ice cream.

NUTRITION FACTS: 3 tablespoons sauce (calculated without ice cream) equals 64 calories, trace fat (trace saturated fat), 0 cholesterol, 33 mg sodium, 16 g carbohydrate, trace fiber, trace protein. DIABETIC EXCHANGE: 1 starch.

down-home dinner

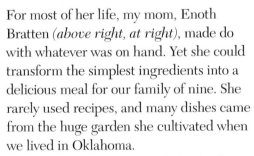

By Ginny Werkmeister
Tilden, Nebraska

For most of her life, my mom, Enoth Bratten (*above right, at right*), made do with whatever was on hand. Yet she could transform the simplest ingredients into a delicious meal for our family of nine. She rarely used recipes, and many dishes came from the huge garden she cultivated when we lived in Oklahoma.

During those years, my dad, Ulis, farmed but also worked in the aircraft industry to make ends meet. Mom stayed home and helped with the finances by raising chickens and turkeys, selling eggs and canning everything her garden produced. We kids helped her with gardening and cooking.

By age 8, I was already whipping up batches of brownies, corn bread and biscuits. "A really good biscuit makes a slim meal more pleasing," Mom would say, and I agree!

On Sundays, Mom often served Fried Chicken with Pan Gravy, Creamed Potatoes & Peas, Garden Coleslaw and Coconut Cream Angel Pie. For years, she made this marvelous meal with antiquated kitchen tools and an old stove.

My parents gave up the farm when I was 13, and Mom became a beautician. Our lives changed again when we moved to southern California, where Mom cut hair for young starlets and I went to high school.

When I married my husband, Marvin, we ended up on a Nebraska farm, where we raised three children. I ran a small greenhouse business and loved every minute because I truly am my mother's daughter.

on the menu
Fried Chicken with Pan Gravy
Creamed Potatoes & Peas
Garden Coleslaw
Coconut Cream Angel Pie

Coconut Cream Angel Pie

PREP: 30 MINUTES
BAKE: 20 MINUTES + CHILLING
YIELD: 8 SERVINGS

- 1/2 cup sugar
- 1/4 cup cornstarch
- 1/4 teaspoon salt
- 2 cups milk
- 3 egg yolks, lightly beaten
- 1/2 cup flaked coconut
- 1 tablespoon butter
- 1 1/2 teaspoons vanilla extract
- 1 pastry shell (9 inches), baked

MERINGUE

- 3 egg whites
- 1/4 teaspoon cream of tartar
- 1/4 teaspoon vanilla extract
- 6 tablespoons sugar
- 1/4 cup flaked coconut

1. In a small heavy saucepan, combine the sugar, cornstarch and salt. Add the milk; stir until smooth. Cook and stir over medium-high heat until thickened and bubbly. Reduce heat to low; cook and stir for 2 minutes longer.

2. Remove from the heat. Stir a small amount of the hot filling into the egg yolks; return all to the pan, stirring constantly. Bring to a gentle boil; cook and stir 2 minutes longer. Remove from the heat; stir in the coconut, butter and vanilla. Pour into the prepared pastry shell.

3. In a small bowl, beat the egg whites, cream of tartar and vanilla on medium speed until soft peaks form. Gradually beat in the sugar, 1 tablespoon at a time, on high until stiff peaks form. Spread the meringue over the hot filling, sealing the edges to the crust. Sprinkle with coconut.

4. Bake at 350° for 20 minutes or until golden brown. Cool on a wire rack for 1 hour; refrigerate for 1-2 hours before serving.

Fried Chicken with Pan Gravy

PREP: 15 MINUTES
COOK: 30 MINUTES
YIELD: 6 SERVINGS (1-1/2 CUPS GRAVY)

- 1 cup all-purpose flour
- 3/4 teaspoon salt
- 1/4 teaspoon dried thyme
- 1/4 teaspoon rubbed sage
- 1/4 teaspoon pepper
- 1 broiler/fryer chicken (3 1/2 to 4 pounds), cut up

Oil for frying

GRAVY

- 2 tablespoons all-purpose flour
- 1/8 teaspoon salt
- 1 1/3 cups milk

1. In a large resealable plastic bag, combine the first five ingredients. Add chicken, a few pieces at a time, and shake to coat.

2. In a large skillet over medium-high heat, heat 1/4 in. of oil; fry chicken until browned on all sides. Reduce heat; cover and cook for 30-35 minutes or until juices run clear, turning occasionally. Uncover and cook 5 minutes longer. Remove chicken to paper towels and keep warm.

3. For gravy, pour off excess fat from skillet, reserving the browned bits and 2 tablespoons drippings. Stir in the flour and salt until blended; gradually add the milk. Bring to a boil; cook and stir for 1-2 minutes or until thickened. Serve gravy with chicken.

Creamed Potatoes & Peas

PREP: 10 MINUTES
COOK: 25 MINUTES
YIELD: 6 SERVINGS

1 pound small red potatoes
2 1/2 cups frozen peas
1/4 cup butter, cubed
1 green onion, sliced
1/4 cup all-purpose flour
1/2 teaspoon salt
Dash pepper
2 cups milk

1. Scrub and quarter the red potatoes; place in a large saucepan and cover with water. Bring to a boil. Reduce heat; cover and simmer for 10 minutes. Add the peas; cook 5 minutes longer or until the potatoes and peas are tender.

2. Meanwhile, in another large saucepan, melt butter. Add onion; saute until tender. Stir in the flour, salt and pepper until blended; gradually add the milk.

3. Bring to a boil. Cook and stir for 1-2 minutes or until thickened. Drain potatoes and peas; toss with sauce.

Garden Coleslaw

PREP/TOTAL TIME: 10 MINUTES
YIELD: 4 SERVINGS

3 cups shredded cabbage
1/4 cup chopped green pepper
1 green onion, thinly sliced
1/4 cup mayonnaise
1/4 cup heavy whipping cream
1 teaspoon sugar
1 teaspoon cider vinegar
1/4 teaspoon salt

1. In a small bowl, combine the cabbage, green pepper and green onion. Combine the remaining ingredients; add to the cabbage mixture and toss to coat.

CABBAGE CLUES

- Look for heads of cabbage with crisp leaves that are firmly packed. The head should feel heavy for its size.
- Store cabbage tightly wrapped in a plastic bag in the refrigerator for up to 2 weeks.
- Remove the core, rinse the cabbage and blot it dry just before using.
- To core a cabbage, cut it in half or quarters. Then make a V-shaped cut around the core and remove it.
- To shred cabbage by hand, cut it into wedges. Place the cut side down on a cutting board. With a large sharp knife, cut it into thin slices.

food is a family affair

By Paula Montijo
Lebanon, Pennsylvania

By the age of 10, my mom, Nancy Kreiser *(above right, at right)*, was taking on much of the cooking so her parents could work the farm.

Even after Mom married my dad, Paul, and had four children, they helped on the farm and kept a garden. I remember our freezer always stocked with beef, corn and strawberries, and the basement shelves lined with jars of canned vegetables and fruit.

When we were kids, my mother had a delicious dinner on the table every night, and we enjoyed eating together as a family.

Beef Roast with Gravy is a main course I always asked Mom to fix for special occasions—and not just for the taste. I loved to smell the aroma as it cooked.

Mom's Honey Sweet Corn is such a treat, especially in summer. The honey butter makes the ears even sweeter.

When zucchini is in season, Mom likes to make crisp, tangy Zucchini Relish.

Fresh-baked desserts were a staple. We loved the strawberries and cream filling in delectable Cake Roll with Berries.

We have a standing invitation for Sunday dinner. Although Mom can no longer do the cooking herself for health reasons, she supervises Dad and us girls.

We all pitch in on the canning, too, as Mom supervises. My dad and brother pick fruit so Dad can freeze it or make jelly to share, which delights the 10 grandkids.

Now I enjoy making Mom's special recipes for my husband and our children.

on the menu
Beef Roast with Gravy
Zucchini Relish
Honey Sweet Corn
Cake Roll with Berries

Beef Roast with Gravy

PREP: 10 MINUTES
COOK: 6 HOURS
YIELD: 8 SERVINGS

- 1 pound fresh baby carrots
- 1 can (4 ounces) mushroom stems and pieces, drained
- 1 beef rump roast or bottom round roast (3 pounds)
- 1/2 teaspoon garlic powder
- 1/4 teaspoon pepper
- 1 tablespoon canola oil
- 1 jar (12 ounces) beef gravy
- 1 can (10 3/4 ounces) condensed cream of mushroom soup, undiluted
- 1 cup water
- 1 envelope onion soup mix

1. Place the carrots and mushrooms in a 4- or 5-qt. slow cooker. Sprinkle roast with garlic powder and pepper. In a large skillet, brown roast in oil on all sides. Transfer to slow cooker.

2. Combine the beef gravy, cream of mushroom soup, water and onion soup mix; pour over the roast. Cover and cook on low for 6-8 hours or until meat is tender. Skim fat from gravy if necessary; serve gravy with beef.

My Mom's Best Meal

Zucchini Relish

PREP: 20 MINUTES + STANDING
COOK: 15 MINUTES + CHILLING
YIELD: 4 CUPS

- 4 cups diced zucchini
- 1 large onion, thinly sliced
- 2 celery ribs, sliced
- 2 medium carrots, sliced
- 1 medium sweet red pepper, sliced
- 2 tablespoons salt
- 3/4 cup sugar
- 1/2 cup water
- 1/2 cup cider vinegar
- 1/2 teaspoon celery seed
- Dash onion salt
- Dash ground turmeric

1. In a large bowl, combine the vegetables; sprinkle with salt and cover with cold water. Let stand for 3 hours; rinse and drain.

2. In a large saucepan, bring the remaining ingredients to a boil. Stir in zucchini mixture and return to a boil. Reduce heat; simmer, uncovered, for 5 minutes. Transfer to a large bowl; cool to room temperature. Cover and refrigerate for at least 2 days.

Honey Sweet Corn

PREP/TOTAL TIME: 15 MINUTES
YIELD: 6 SERVINGS

 6 medium ears sweet corn
 1/4 cup butter, melted
 1 teaspoon honey
Ground pepper, optional

1. Place the corn in a Dutch oven or stockpot; cover with water. Bring to a boil; cover and cook for 5-10 minutes or until tender. Drain. In a small bowl, combine butter and honey; brush over corn. Sprinkle with pepper if desired.

Cake Roll with Berries

PREP: 40 MINUTES
BAKE: 15 MINUTES + CHILLING
YIELD: 10 SERVINGS

 3 eggs
 1 cup sugar
 1/3 cup water
 1 teaspoon vanilla extract
 3/4 cup all-purpose flour
 1 teaspoon baking powder
 1/4 teaspoon salt
Confectioners' sugar

FILLING
 1/2 cup all-purpose flour
 1 cup milk
 1/2 cup butter, softened
 1/2 cup shortening
 1 cup sugar
 1 teaspoon vanilla extract
 1/4 teaspoon salt

BERRIES
 3 cups sliced fresh strawberries
 1/4 cup sugar

1. Line a greased 15-in. x 10-in. x 1-in. baking pan with waxed paper and grease the paper; set aside.

2. In a large bowl, beat eggs on high speed for 3 minutes. Gradually add sugar, beating until mixture becomes thick and lemon-colored. Beat in water and vanilla. Combine the flour, baking powder and salt; fold into egg mixture. Spread batter into prepared pan.

3. Bake at 375° for 12-15 minutes or until cake springs back when lightly touched. Cool for 5 minutes. Invert onto a kitchen towel dusted with confectioners' sugar. Gently peel off waxed paper. Roll up cake in the towel jelly-roll style, starting with a short side. Cool completely on a wire rack.

4. Meanwhile, for filling, combine flour and milk in a small saucepan until smooth. Cook and stir over medium heat until mixture comes to a boil; cook and stir 2 minutes longer (mixture will be very thick). Transfer to a bowl; press waxed paper onto surface of mixture. Cool completely.

5. In a large bowl, cream the butter, shortening and sugar until light and fluffy. Beat in vanilla and salt. Gradually beat in milk mixture; beat for 5 minutes or until filling is light and fluffy.

6. Unroll cake; spread filling over cake to within 1/2 in. of edges. Roll up again. Place seam side down on a serving platter. Sprinkle with confectioners' sugar. Combine strawberries and sugar; refrigerate cake and berries for 1 hour before serving.

perfect for picnics

By Kim Wallace
Dennison, Ohio

For as long as I can remember, my mom, Bertha Meese *(above right, at left)*, has spent much of her time in the kitchen preparing meals for family, friends, business associates and others. When my brother, Billy, and I were kids, we sat down to her home-cooked dinners every night.

Good cooking has been passed down in our family from generation to generation. My grandmother and great-grandmother shared their skills with Mom and then me. I hope to pass on what I've learned to my two daughters and one son as well.

There's only one problem: Few things Mom makes have a recipe! She cooks from scratch, using a pinch of this and a dash of that, with a smattering of several other ingredients tossed in for good measure.

The meal I've shared here wins rave reviews with the whole family—and I have the recipes! The menu starts with saucy Barbecued Pork Sandwiches, great for a hungry crowd and easy to prepare. Once the meat is cooked, transfer it to a slow cooker to keep it warm until serving time.

I always use the recipe for Dad's Baked Beans when I need baked beans for any occasion; they're the best I've ever had. And crunchy Campers' Coleslaw is a traditional, no-fuss slaw that makes a refreshing side dish for summer picnics and parties.

With its light, golden crust and yummy filling, Cream Puff Cake is a definite crowd-pleaser. Be prepared for recipe requests!

on the menu
Barbecued Pork Sandwiches
Dad's Baked Beans
Campers' Coleslaw
Cream Puff Cake

Barbecued Pork Sandwiches

PREP: 25 MINUTES
COOK: 2-1/2 HOURS
YIELD: 10 SERVINGS

- 1 boneless pork shoulder butt roast (3 pounds)
- 1 medium onion, chopped
- 1 tablespoon butter
- 1 can (15 ounces) tomato puree
- 1/2 cup packed brown sugar
- 1/4 cup Worcestershire sauce
- 2 tablespoons lemon juice
- 1/2 teaspoon salt
- 10 hard rolls, split

1. Place pork on a rack in a roasting pan; bake, uncovered, at 350° for 2 hours or until tender.

2. In a Dutch oven, saute onion in butter until tender. Stir in the tomato puree, brown sugar, Worcestershire sauce, lemon juice and salt. Bring to a boil. Reduce heat; simmer, uncovered, for 30 minutes. Shred the pork; add to the sauce and heat through. Serve on buns.

My Mom's Best Meal

Dad's Baked Beans

PREP: 15 MINUTES
BAKE: 1 HOUR
YIELD: 8 SERVINGS

- 3 cans (15 1/2 ounces each) great northern beans, rinsed and drained
- 5 hot dogs, sliced
- 1 1/2 cups ketchup
- 1/2 cup packed brown sugar
- 2 tablespoons molasses
- 1 medium onion, chopped
- 1/2 teaspoon ground mustard
- 1/4 teaspoon salt
- 1/4 teaspoon pepper

1. In an ungreased 2-quart baking dish, combine all ingredients. Cover and bake at 350° for 1 to 1-1/2 hours or until heated through.

GOING DUTCH

A Dutch oven can easily go from stovetop to oven to table. If you worry that your food will stick to the pot, heat it over medium heat before adding the food. To clean a Dutch oven, fill it with water and boil it until the food releases. Drain the water and scrub with a ball of aluminum foil to remove any burned-on food.

Campers' Coleslaw

PREP: 20 MINUTES + CHILLING
YIELD: 12 SERVINGS (3/4 CUP EACH)

- 1 1/2 cups sugar
- 3/4 cup white vinegar
- 3/4 cup olive oil
- 3 teaspoons salt
- 1 teaspoon celery seed
- 1 medium head cabbage, shredded
- 1 large onion, chopped
- 1 medium green pepper, chopped

1. In a small saucepan, combine the first five ingredients. Bring to a boil; boil for 1-2 minutes or until the sugar is dissolved. Remove from the heat; cool to room temperature.

2. In a large bowl, combine the cabbage, onion and pepper; add dressing and toss to coat. Refrigerate until chilled. Serve with a slotted spoon.

NUTRITION FACTS: 3/4 cup equals 121 calories, 6 g fat (1 g saturated fat), 0 cholesterol, 274 mg sodium, 17 g carbohydrate, 2 g fiber, 1 g protein. DIABETIC EXCHANGES: 1 starch, 1 fat.

Cream Puff Cake

PREP: 25 MINUTES
BAKE: 25 MINUTES + CHILLING
YIELD: 15 SERVINGS

1	cup water
1/2	cup butter, cubed
1	cup all-purpose flour
4	eggs

FILLING

1	package (8 ounces) cream cheese, softened
2 1/2	cups 2% milk
3	packages (3.3 ounces each) instant white chocolate or vanilla pudding mix
1	carton (8 ounces) frozen whipped topping, thawed

1. In a large saucepan, bring the water and butter to a boil. Add the flour all at once and stir until a smooth ball forms. Continue beating until the mixture is smooth and shiny.

2. Remove the mixture from the heat; let stand for 5 minutes. Add the eggs, one at a time, beating well after each addition.

3. Transfer to a greased 13-in. x 9-in. baking dish. Bake at 400° for 22-26 minutes or until puffed and golden brown. Cool completely on a wire rack.

4. For the filling, in a large bowl, beat the cream cheese, milk and white chocolate pudding mixes until smooth. Spread over the baked crust; refrigerate for 20 minutes. Spread with whipped topping. Chill until serving.

HER ITALIAN MOTHER COOKED ALMOST EVERYTHING FROM SCRATCH AND NEVER USED RECIPES. THE RESULT? ALWAYS AN ABUNDANCE OF FOOD...AND ROOM FOR ONE MORE AT THE DINNER TABLE.

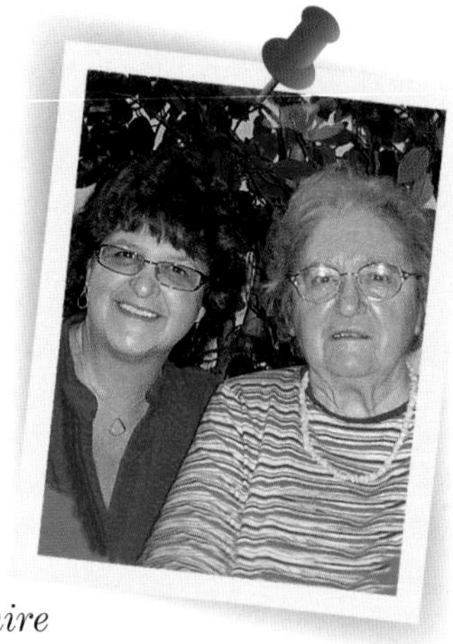

Italian-style dinner

By Linda Harrington
Hudson, New Hampshire

"Are you hungry?" Those are usually among the first words Italians will utter when you enter their homes.

My mother, Elsie Laurenzo Palmer *(above right, at right)*, from Mechanicville, New York, was no different. Mom used to say, "We always have enough food for anyone who comes to visit."

One of Mom's best holiday dinners started with Italian Christmas Turkey, which featured a favorite of mine—Mom's incredible sausage stuffing.

There was always plenty of Mom's Italian Bread, too. I think she used to bake at least four of these tender loaves at once, and they never lasted long.

Lemon Broccoli with Garlic was an easy, zesty way to use up leftover broccoli.

It was a tradition to have Iced Anise Cookies on hand for Thanksgiving, Christmas and Easter.

After my sister, brother and I started school, Mom worked as an executive secretary at a paper company. My dad, Louis, was a factory worker. As the oldest child, I was responsible for making dinner. On weekends, Mom cooked, and I'd watch and help her. That's how I learned to cook.

I've always enjoyed making Mom's specialties for my husband, Jim, three grown daughters and two grandchildren.

More than the wonderful taste and aroma of Mom's cooking, I cherish the memories of our family gathered around the dinner table.

on the menu

Italian Christmas Turkey
Lemon Broccoli with Garlic
Mom's Italian Bread
Iced Anise Cookies

Italian Christmas Turkey

PREP: 40 MINUTES
BAKE: 3-3/4 HOURS + STANDING
YIELD: 16 SERVINGS (12 CUPS STUFFING)

1/2 cup butter, cubed
1 pound bulk Italian sausage
2 celery ribs, chopped
1 medium onion, chopped
1 package (14 ounces) seasoned stuffing cubes
1/4 cup egg substitute
2 to 3 cups hot water
1 turkey (16 pounds)
Salt and pepper to taste

1. In a large skillet over medium heat, melt butter. Add the sausage, celery and onion; cook and stir until meat is no longer pink. Transfer to a large bowl; stir in the stuffing cubes, egg substitute and enough hot water to reach desired moistness.

2. Just before baking, loosely stuff turkey with stuffing. Place remaining stuffing in a greased 2-qt. baking dish; cover and refrigerate. Remove from the refrigerator 30 minutes before baking.

3. Skewer turkey openings; tie drumsticks together. Place breast side up in a roasting pan. Rub with salt and pepper.

4. Bake, uncovered, at 325° for 3-3/4 to 4-1/4 hours or until a meat thermometer reads 180° for turkey and 165° for stuffing, basting occasionally with pan drippings. (Cover loosely with foil if turkey browns too quickly.)

5. Bake additional stuffing, covered, for 25-30 minutes. Uncover; bake 10 minutes longer or until a thermometer reads 160°. Cover turkey and let stand for 20 minutes before removing stuffing and carving turkey. If desired, thicken pan drippings for gravy.

My Mom's Best Meal

Lemon Broccoli
with Garlic

PREP/TOTAL TIME: 20 MINUTES
YIELD: 6 SERVINGS

1   large bunch broccoli, cut into florets
1/2 cup olive oil
1/4 cup lemon juice
4   garlic cloves, minced
1/4 teaspoon salt
1/8 teaspoon pepper

1. Place broccoli in a steamer basket; place in a large saucepan over 1 in. of water. Bring to a boil; cover and steam for 6-8 minutes or until crisp-tender.

2. Meanwhile, in a small bowl, combine the remaining ingredients. Immediately place broccoli in ice water. Drain and pat dry. Place in a large bowl. Pour oil mixture over broccoli; toss to coat. Refrigerate until serving.

Mom's Italian Bread

PREP: 30 MINUTES + RISING
BAKE: 20 MINUTES + COOLING
YIELD: 2 LOAVES (12 SLICES EACH)

- 1 package (1/4 ounce) active dry yeast
- 2 cups warm water (110° to 115°)
- 1 teaspoon sugar
- 2 teaspoons salt
- 5 1/2 cups all-purpose flour

1. In a large bowl, dissolve yeast in warm water. Add the sugar, salt and 3 cups flour. Beat on medium speed for 3 minutes. Stir in remaining flour to form soft dough.

2. Turn onto a floured surface; knead until smooth and elastic, about 6-8 minutes. Place in a greased bowl, turning once to grease the top. Cover and let rise in a warm place until doubled, about 1 hour.

3. Punch dough down. Turn onto a floured surface; divide in half. Shape each portion into a loaf. Place each loaf seam side down on a greased baking sheet. Cover and let rise until doubled, about 30 minutes. With a sharp knife, make four shallow slashes across top of each loaf.

4. Bake at 400° for 20-25 minutes or until golden brown. Remove from pans to wire racks to cool.

Iced Anise Cookies

PREP: 45 MINUTES
BAKE: 10 MINUTES/BATCH
YIELD: 6 DOZEN

- 2 2/3 cups all-purpose flour
- 1/2 cup sugar
- 3 teaspoons baking powder
- 3 eggs
- 1/2 cup butter, melted
- 1/4 cup 2% milk
- 2 teaspoons anise extract

ICING
- 1/4 cup butter, softened
- 2 cups confectioners' sugar
- 3 tablespoons 2% milk
- 1/2 teaspoon lemon extract
Coarse and colored sugars, optional

1. In a large bowl, combine 2 cups flour, sugar and baking powder. In a small bowl, whisk the eggs, butter, milk and extract. Stir into dry ingredients until blended. Stir in remaining flour until dough forms a ball. Turn onto a floured surface; knead until smooth.

2. Shape dough by rounded teaspoonfuls into thin 6-in. ropes; twist each rope into a "Q" shape. Place on ungreased baking sheets. Bake at 350° for 8-10 minutes or until set. Remove from pans to wire racks to cool completely.

3. For the icing, in a small bowl, beat the butter until fluffy. Add the confectioners' sugar, milk and lemon extract; beat until smooth. Spread over the tops of the cookies; decorate with coarse and colored sugars if desired.

fresh farm fare

By Gayleen Grote
Battleview, North Dakota

Growing up on a farm in North Dakota, meals were an important part of the day. My father, Ray, was a farmer/rancher before retiring, and I'd help out in the fields.

No matter what time we got home, Mom, Eunice Tangsrud *(above right)*, would have a big meal waiting for us. This supper is one I love to this day.

Alongside the Creamed Peas and Carrots, the crunchy, breaded Pan-Fried Venison tastes amazing. This recipe was always a top choice if we had deer meat on hand.

Because my brother was allergic to milk, Mom created her tender Perfect Dinner Rolls. They absolutely melt in your mouth!

Frozen Strawberry Dessert is a pretty pink treat that's so refreshing after a hearty dinner. The fruity whipped cream filling is sandwiched between a crumbly pecan crust and topping.

My brother and I learned at an early age to appreciate whatever food was put before us. That was easy with Mom's delicious home cooking!

I don't remember Mom "teaching" me to cook; as a child, I usually wanted to spend more time outdoors than in the kitchen. When I got older, however, I'd call Mom and ask her how to do something.

Now, I cook for my husband, Scott, and our three children—Allison, Karla and Brandon. I love those special moments of working with the kids in the kitchen.

on the menu
Pan-Fried Venison Steak
Perfect Dinner Rolls
Creamed Peas and Carrots
Frozen Strawberry Dessert

pan-fried venison steak
RECIPE ON PAGE 196

My Mom's Best Meal

195

Pan-Fried Venison Steak

PREP/TOTAL TIME: 25 MINUTES
YIELD: 4 SERVINGS

- 1   pound venison or beef tenderloin, cut into 1/2-inch slices
- 2   cups crushed saltines
- 2   eggs
- 3/4 cup milk
- 1   teaspoon salt
- 1/2 teaspoon pepper
- 5   tablespoons vegetable oil

1. Flatten venison to 1/4-in. thickness. Place the saltines in a shallow bowl. In another shallow bowl, whisk the eggs, milk, salt and pepper. Coat the venison with the saltines, then dip in the egg mixture and coat a second time with saltines.

2. In a large skillet over medium heat, cook venison in oil in batches for 2-3 minutes on each side or until the meat reaches desired doneness.

Perfect Dinner Rolls

PREP: 30 MINUTES + RISING
BAKE: 15 MINUTES
YIELD: 2 DOZEN

- 1   tablespoon active dry yeast
- 2 1/4 cups warm water (110° to 115°)
- 1/3 cup sugar
- 1/3 cup shortening
- 1/4 cup powdered nondairy creamer
- 2 1/4 teaspoons salt
- 6   to 7 cups bread flour

1. In a large bowl, dissolve yeast in warm water. Add the sugar, shortening, creamer, salt and 5 cups flour. Beat until smooth. Stir in enough remaining flour to form a soft dough (dough will be sticky).

2. Turn the dough onto a floured surface; knead until smooth and elastic, about 6-8 minutes. Place in a bowl coated with cooking spray, turning once to coat the top. Cover and let rise in a warm place until doubled, about 1 hour.

3. Punch the dough down. Turn dough onto a lightly floured surface; divide into 24 pieces. Shape each piece into a roll. Place 2 in. apart on baking sheets coated with cooking spray. Cover and let rise until doubled, about 30 minutes.

4. Bake at 350° for 12-15 minutes or until lightly browned. Remove from pans to wire racks.

FLATTENING MEAT

- Flattening or pounding meat can serve several purposes. It is typically done for quicker, more even cooking and for an attractive appearance.

- When tender cuts of meat or poultry are flattened, it's best to put them inside a heavy-duty resealable plastic bag or between two sheets of heavy plastic wrap to prevent messy splatters. Use only the smooth side of a meat mallet to gently pound them to the desired thickness. This will prevent the meat from shredding.

- When tougher cuts of meat need tenderizing, they are pounded with the ridged side of a meat mallet to break up the connective tissue.

Creamed Peas and Carrots

PREP/TOTAL TIME: 25 MINUTES
YIELD: 4 SERVINGS

- 4 medium carrots, sliced
- 2 cups frozen peas
- 1 tablespoon cornstarch
- 1/4 teaspoon salt
- 1/8 teaspoon pepper
- 1/2 cup heavy whipping cream

1. Place the carrots in a large saucepan; add 1 in. of water. Bring to a boil. Reduce the heat; cover and simmer for 10 minutes.

2. Add the peas; return to a boil. Reduce the heat; cover and simmer 5-10 minutes longer or until vegetables are tender. Drain, reserving 1/2 cup cooking liquid. Return vegetables and reserved liquid to the pan.

3. In a small bowl, combine the cornstarch, salt, pepper and cream until smooth. Stir into vegetables. Bring to a boil; cook and stir for 1-2 minutes or until thickened.

Frozen Strawberry Dessert

PREP: 25 MINUTES + FREEZING
YIELD: 9 SERVINGS

- 1 cup all-purpose flour
- 1/4 cup packed brown sugar
- 1/2 cup cold butter
- 1/2 cup chopped pecans
- 2 cups frozen unsweetened strawberries, thawed
- 1 cup sugar
- 1 teaspoon lemon juice
- 1 cup heavy whipping cream, whipped

1. In a small bowl, combine the flour and brown sugar; cut in the butter until crumbly. Stir in the pecans. Press the mixture into an ungreased 9-in. square baking pan. Bake at 350° for 14-16 minutes or until lightly browned. Cool on a wire rack.

2. Crumble the baked pecan mixture; set aside 1/2 cup for topping. Sprinkle the remaining mixture into an 8-in. square dish.

3. In a large mixing bowl, beat the strawberries, sugar and lemon juice until blended. Fold in whipped cream. Spread evenly into the dish. Sprinkle with the reserved pecan mixture. Cover and freeze dessert for 8 hours or overnight.

AN ABUNDANCE OF HOMEGROWN VEGETABLES AND FRUIT STAR IN HER MOTHER'S WHOLESOME COOKING, PACKED WITH FRESH-PICKED GOODNESS AND MOUTH-WATERING FLAVOR.

grill-side supper

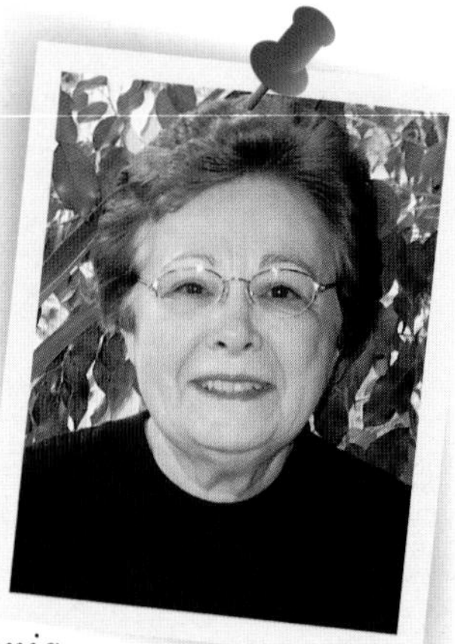

By Kathy Spang
Manheim, Pennsylvania

A love of cooking goes way back for my mom, Clara Kniss *(above right)*. The oldest of five children, Mom learned to cook and bake from her mother and joined the 4-H Cooking Club.

She learned the importance of fresh fruits and vegetables early on. So my sister, Karen, and I grew up enjoying the bounty from our grandparents' farm.

My mother would also freeze and can fruit and veggies so we could enjoy them year-round. We all live nearby, and Mom invites our families over frequently and also hosts extended family for holiday get-togethers and picnics.

Full of fresh flavors, this meal, which I've loved since childhood, reminds me of the farm. Sizzling Beef Kabobs combine marinated beef, squash, onion and peppers. Mom enlists Dad to do the grilling.

My grandfather often requested Mom's Lattice Corn Pie for his birthday. Now I'm passing on this dish and the stories that go with it to my husband, Doug, and our children, Luke and Kate.

The kids especially love Applesauce-Raspberry Gelatin Mold. It's not only cool and refreshing, but easy as well.

My sister learned to make Pavlova from her Australian mother-in-law. Then, Karen taught Mom. Assorted fresh fruits look beautiful on top of this dessert.

What really makes Mom's recipes special are the memories tied to them. And with each new dish she tries, we create even more.

on the menu

Sizzling Beef Kabobs
Pavlova
Applesauce-Raspberry Gelatin Mold
Lattice Corn Pie

lattice corn pie
RECIPE ON PAGE 201

Sizzling Beef Kabobs

PREP: 20 MINUTES + MARINATING
GRILL: 10 MINUTES
YIELD: 8 SERVINGS

1/3	cup canola oil
1/4	cup soy sauce
2	tablespoons red wine vinegar
2	teaspoons garlic powder
2	pounds boneless beef sirloin steak, cut into 1-inch pieces
2	medium yellow summer squash, cut into 1/2-inch slices
1	large onion, cut into 1-inch chunks
1	large green pepper, cut into 1-inch pieces
1	large sweet red pepper, cut into 1-inch pieces

1. In a large resealable plastic bag, combine the oil, soy sauce, vinegar and garlic powder; add beef. Seal bag and turn to coat; refrigerate for at least 1 hour.

2. Drain and discard marinade. On eight metal or soaked wooden skewers, alternately thread beef pieces and vegetables. Grill, covered, over medium-hot heat or broil 4-6 in. from the heat for 8-10 minutes or until the meat reaches desired doneness, turning occasionally.

Pavlova

PREP: 25 MINUTES
BAKE: 45 MINUTES + STANDING
YIELD: 6-8 SERVINGS

4	egg whites
1	teaspoon vanilla extract
1	teaspoon white vinegar
1	cup sugar
1	carton (8 ounces) frozen whipped topping, thawed
2	cups sliced fresh strawberries
2	cups cubed fresh pineapple
2	medium kiwifruit, peeled and sliced

1. Place egg whites in a large mixing bowl; let stand at room temperature for 30 minutes. Beat until foamy.

2. Add vanilla and vinegar; beat until soft peaks form. Gradually beat in the sugar, 1 tablespoon at a time, on high until stiff glossy peaks form and the sugar is dissolved.

3. Spoon the meringue onto a parchment paper-lined baking sheet. Using the back of a spoon, shape into a 9-in. circle. Bake at 225° for 45-55 minutes or until set and dry. Turn the oven off and do not open door. Let meringue dry in oven for 1 hour.

4. Just before serving, top the meringue with whipped topping and fresh fruit. Refrigerate leftovers.

BREAK THE MOLD

- To unmold gelatin, loosen it from the top edge of the mold by gently pulling the gelatin away from the edge with a moistened finger. Then dip the mold up to its rim in a sink or pan of warm water for a few seconds or until the edges begin to release from the side of the mold. Next, place a platter over the mold, invert and carefully lift the mold from the salad.
- When unmolding a large gelatin salad, rinse the platter with cold water before turning the gelatin out. The moisture will allow the unmolded salad to be easily centered on the platter.

Applesauce-Raspberry Gelatin Mold

PREP: 15 MINUTES + CHILLING
YIELD: 10 SERVINGS

- 3 cups unsweetened applesauce
- 1/4 cup orange juice
- 2 packages (3 ounces each) raspberry gelatin
- 1 1/2 cups lemon-lime soda

1. In a large saucepan, bring applesauce and orange juice to a boil. Remove from the heat; stir in the gelatin until dissolved. Slowly add soda.
2. Pour into a 6-cup mold coated with cooking spray. Refrigerate until firm. Unmold onto a serving platter.

NUTRITION FACTS: 1/2 cup equals 111 calories, trace fat (trace saturated fat), 0 cholesterol, 44 mg sodium, 27 g carbohydrate, 1 g fiber, 2 g protein. DIABETIC EXCHANGES: 1 starch, 1/2 fruit.

Lattice Corn Pie

PREP: 25 MINUTES
BAKE: 35 MINUTES
YIELD: 8 SERVINGS

- 1 cup diced peeled potatoes
- 1/3 cup milk
- 2 eggs
- 2 cups fresh or frozen corn, thawed
- 1 teaspoon sugar
- 1/2 teaspoon salt
- 1 package (15 ounces) refrigerated pie pastry

1. Place the potatoes in a small saucepan and cover with water. Bring to a boil. Reduce heat; cover and cook for 6-8 minutes or until tender. Drain and set aside.
2. In a blender, combine the milk, eggs, corn, sugar and salt; cover and process until blended.
3. Line a 9-in. pie plate with bottom pastry; trim the pastry even with edge of plate. Spoon potatoes into crust; top with corn mixture (crust will be full). Roll out the remaining pastry; make a lattice crust. Seal and flute the edges.
4. Bake at 375° for 35-40 minutes or until the crust is golden brown and filling is bubbly.

from-the-sea favorite

By Mary Lou Boyce
Wilmington, Delaware

For seven generations, farming was the only life our family knew. My mother, Mildred Derickson Woodward *(above right)*, married a dairy farmer. I grew up on the farm along with my two brothers.

Mom fed Dad and us kids three "square meals" a day. She cooked everything from scratch, and we ate whatever was put in front of us. Picky eaters were simply not tolerated at the table!

The menu I chose as Mom's best is one of my all-time favorites—nutritious, tasty and simple to make.

Flavored with cheddar cheese and salad dressing, Caesar Orange Roughy is fork-tender, with a crunchy coating. Buttery and homey Creamed Mushrooms, to me, are real comfort food.

Mom used produce from our huge vegetable garden to make dishes like tangy Cucumber Salad and speedy Glazed Julienned Carrots. She also relied on fruit from the orchards, along with the beef, chicken and pork we raised.

One of my fondest memories is of coming home from school with my brothers to the aroma of Ranger Cookies baking.

My grandmother was the one who taught me to make bread when I was 8 years old… my introduction to cooking. But Mom inspired me to cook. She was a loving, caring and devoted person. I hope you'll be inspired to try her delicious meal.

on the menu
Caesar Orange Roughy
Glazed Julienned Carrots
Creamed Mushrooms
Cucumber Salad
Ranger Cookies

caesar orange roughy
RECIPE ON PAGE 204

My Mom's Best Meal

Glazed Julienned Carrots

PREP/TOTAL TIME: 20 MINUTES
YIELD: 8 SERVINGS

- 2 pounds carrots, julienned
- 1/3 cup butter, cubed
- 1/4 cup sugar
- 1/4 cup water
- 1/2 teaspoon salt

1. In a large skillet, combine all ingredients. Cover and cook over medium heat for 7-10 minutes or until the carrots are crisp-tender. Serve with a slotted spoon.

Caesar Orange Roughy

PREP/TOTAL TIME: 25 MINUTES
YIELD: 8 SERVINGS

- 2 pounds fresh or frozen orange roughy fillets, thawed
- 1 cup Caesar salad dressing
- 2 cups crushed butter-flavored crackers (about 50 crackers)
- 1 cup (4 ounces) shredded cheddar cheese

1. Place fillets in an ungreased 13-in. x 9-in. x 2-in. baking dish. Drizzle with Caesar salad dressing; sprinkle with cracker crumbs.

2. Bake, uncovered, at 400° for 10 minutes. Sprinkle with cheddar cheese. Bake 3-5 minutes longer or until the fish flakes easily with a fork and the cheese is melted.

Creamed Mushrooms

PREP/TOTAL TIME: 25 MINUTES
YIELD: 8 SERVINGS

- 3 pounds sliced fresh mushrooms
- 1/2 cup butter, cubed
- 1/2 cup all-purpose flour
- 2 1/2 cups milk
- 1 cup evaporated milk
- 2 teaspoons salt

1. Place mushrooms in a large kettle; cover with water. Bring to a boil; stir. Reduce heat; cover and simmer for 3 minutes or until tender. Drain well.

2. In a Dutch oven, melt the butter. Stir in the flour until smooth; gradually add milk and evaporated milk. Bring to a boil; cook and stir for 2 minutes or until thickened. Stir in the salt and mushrooms. Cook and stir over medium heat for 3-4 minutes or until heated through.

Cucumber Salad

PREP: 15 MINUTES + CHILLING
YIELD: 8-10 SERVINGS

- 7 cups thinly sliced peeled cucumbers
- 2 cups sugar
- 1 large onion, chopped
- 1 medium green pepper, chopped
- 1 cup cider vinegar
- 1 tablespoon salt
- 1 tablespoon celery seed

1. In a large serving bowl, combine all ingredients. Cover and refrigerate for at least 1 hour, stirring occasionally. Serve salad with a slotted spoon.

Ranger Cookies

PREP: 25 MINUTES
BAKE: 10 MINUTES/BATCH
YIELD: 7-1/2 DOZEN

- 1 cup shortening
- 1 cup sugar
- 1 cup packed brown sugar
- 2 eggs
- 1 teaspoon vanilla extract
- 2 cups all-purpose flour
- 1 teaspoon baking soda
- 1/2 teaspoon baking powder
- 1/2 teaspoon salt
- 2 cups quick-cooking oats
- 2 cups crisp rice cereal
- 1 cup flaked coconut

1. In a large mixing bowl, cream shortening and sugars until light and fluffy. Beat in the eggs and vanilla. Combine the flour, baking soda, baking powder and salt; gradually add to creamed mixture and mix well. Stir in the oats, cereal and coconut.

2. Drop dough by rounded tablespoonfuls 2 in. apart onto ungreased baking sheets. Bake at 350° for 7-9 minutes or until golden brown. Remove to wire racks.

my own food memories